# Suspended

## Travels Close to Home

## Pete Sarsfield

Pottersfield Press, Lawrencetown Beach, Nova Scotia, Canada

National Library of Canada Cataloguing in Publication

Sarsfield, Pete, 1944-

    Suspended : travels close to home / Pete Sarsfield.

ISBN 1-895900-58-1

1. Sarsfield, Pete, 1944– — Journeys.  2. Canada — Description and travel — 1981– — Guidebooks.  I. Title.

FC75.S37 2003     917.104'648     C2003-904315-0

**Cover design:** Dalhousie Graphics

**Cover and author's photo:** Tom Thomson

Pottersfield Press acknowledges the support of the Canada Council for the Arts which last year invested $20.3 million in writing and publishing throughout Canada. We acknowledge the financial support of the Government of Canada through the Book Publishing Industry Development Program for our publishing activities. We also acknowledge the support of the Nova Scotia Department of Tourism and Culture, Cultural Affairs Division.

Pottersfield Press
83 Leslie Road
East Lawrencetown
Nova Scotia, Canada, B2Z 1P8
Website: www.pottersfieldpress.com
To order, phone toll-free 1-800-NIMBUS9 (1-800-646-2879)
Printed in Canada

*Running with the Caribou* (Turnstone Press 2000)
*Hollow Water* (Turnstone Press 1997)

"I enjoyed this book [*Hollow Water*] for its humour and its honesty."
— Joyce Atcheson, in *The Kenora Enterprise*

"If loose ends bother you, *Running with the Caribou* is not for you."
— Bryan Phelan, in *The Kenora Enterprise*

"A talented pain in the ass . . ."
— Richard Schabas, in conversation

". . . you can write prose that rings with the beauty of good poetry, spare and full . . ."
— Ed Belzer, in a letter

". . . this is a man who is having fun . . ."
— Brian Cameron, in the *Canadian Medical Association Journal*

". . . I hear your voice as I read, and sense your humour, and share your healthy anger . . ."
— Ali Squire, in a letter

"He is opinionated, but not pretentious."
— Karen Green in *Connect!*

"He describes his own thoughts with the same detachment he brings to his experiences with others."
— Linda Turk, in Thunder Bay's *Chronicle-Journal*

"You simply say the way things are, and that pleases me more than anything."
— Jodi Essery, in a letter

"I'd like to live in Pete Sarsfield's brain — but only for a little while."
— Molly Mason, in the *Wawatay News*

# Contents

# Mobility

*for Sarah  for Jan*

*"'Suspended' . . . the moment in time of getting to the
top of a movement, the edge of it, fulfilling it . . .
leading into further movement."*

*– Jan, at Banff*

*"You make up memories. . . ."*

*– Sarah,
at a Winnipeg  restaurant,
with a forgiving grin*

# Acknowledgements and Thanks

to Karen Sinclair, for dealing with the words and the writer, and for straightening some while allowing others to be crooked;

to sisters Sue and Lisa, brother Mark, and adopted-mother Terry, who are central and hopefully know that I know;

to Alexandria Patience, Christy Barnes, and Monica Meneghetti at the Banff Centre, for offering space in Peter Hemingway's circular totem vision of a Leighton Studio; and to Susan Serran and crew at Toronto Island's Gibraltar Point Centre for the Arts, for the rooms and the island and the neighbours;

to Gail Bull at the Sunshine Coast Festival, for not being offended by brazen self-promotion;

to Ingy and Ed, for enhancing and stabilizing the periphery, and for caring;

to CB, Nigel, Ali, Penny, Koop, KO, Heather, Janet, Kay, Shirley, Mary, Suzanne, Jane, TMS, Bob, Bill, KE, and Johnny G, for allowing us to care, with only occasional revisions;

and to Benita Cohen, frequent companion and all-the-time friend of the heart.

*Pete Sarsfield*
*Kenora, Ontario*
*July 5, 2003*

# Going Back

*"But there is no going back in time
to do anything about it now
if something wasn't done then
and nothing was . . ."*

*— Al Purdy,*
*On Being Human*

*"I breathe carefully, a little at a time, and
dance very rarely. When walking, I hold my
ribs and look steadily behind me."*

*— Erik Satie,*
*A Day in the Life of a Musician*

# *Something Between –*
# *Suspended*

*L*orna Crozier's words are providing context to the Winnipeg Folk Festival. I'm reading her poems *What the Living Won't Let Go* between sets of music, and between wandering the grounds at Bird's Hill Park, watching things happen. There are 25,000 people here today, and I don't feel crowded. It is 30°C in full sun, but I don't feel too warm. I'm alternately alone or with loved ones and acquaintances, and both ways are acceptable. These things are either very straightforward or very complicated, and I never know which one, or if it's always both.

\* \* \*

It rained lightly early last evening, and then overnight it poured. The connection between sky and land is dramatic, as today we have washed green and running mud, evaporating puddles and personal adjustments. It seems, for a few days, that we *are* capable of adapting to the land, as we once had to and did, instead of forcing the land to shift to our awkward shape.

∗   ∗   ∗

The baton is being passed, you can see it happening here, and I hope none of us drops it. The aging hippies, we children of rock music and foreign war, and of new sex and new drugs and long hair, are handing the time-stick to the children of new music and shifting wars, fearful drugs and rules of sex, and blue hair. We have to be careful on the handover, the dangerous time, before one stops altogether and the other shifts into full flight.

∗   ∗   ∗

A friend in Labrador embraces her perception that everything is a metaphor and that this double reality enhances our consistent ability to raise ashes from ashes. The Folk Festival is an ashy metaphor for me, as well as a shifting and overlapping set of realities. For some time I have been suspended, caught by the rocky hard places of past and present and, as a result, unable (or unwilling) to take responsibility for myself, past and present.

I wander off to the small stage called Shady Grove. I'm feeling fed-up and sour, so I don't get the usual dry inner chuckle from the self-mocking irony regarding groves of shades. I go to the back of the clearing where overhanging trees give a break from the scathing prairie sun. Not yet on top of this movement, not having fulfilled it, I can't get to further movement. I look around the grove at the audience, most seated on grass and a few leaving or coming, and watch the small stage to the inclined front. I used to come here with ex-partner Rene and our twin daughters Jan and Sarah. Now they don't, not often.

Rene and I had been together from our teens, from Nova Scotia to Labrador to the Arctic to Winnipeg to alienation and departure.

*12*

We shared music in many places and ways, as listeners, but now she doesn't come here. Jan and Sarah also find this place difficult, laced with sadness, as are many locations, times, songs, and memories. As much as I reject the ill-logic of guilt, recognizing that I have had to work, and hard, to rehabilitate the past and memories and meta-phors, I find that I easily sink into complete self-blame. Their pain and loss becomes my fault, and there is nothing to be done. I under-stand that the nothing-to-be-done part is only true for other people's actions; they *can* do something about it, if they want to work at it. I can do something about my part, only mine.

I get up from the shade and go to look for my friend, Ben, who deserves better than a sour, haunted companion. Perhaps I need to want to do something about that, and to work harder at it.

\* \* \*

Later, I'm lying on my back in the sun, listening to women singing with cheer about men being brutal, dumb, unnecessary, doomed, bald, and in need of erection-enhancing drugs. They don't sing about the connections. This harmonious tone and between-song chatter goes on and on, to great hilarity. I've heard many equally of-fensive anti-female songs and banter from men in the past, so chalk up this pathetic "feminist" sexism to pendulum politics, crude but apparently necessary in order to get the damned thing near balance, near a sensible centre that may hold.

I've noticed two people a few metres of crowded grass away who are also not laughing, and they may be people I used to know, I can't tell for sure. It does help to keep one's eyes closed at certain times. After a while, a shadow passes over my face, then another, and when I look up later, after the obligatory musical ugliness has run its course, and the two old-lost acquaintances or never-found strangers are gone.

Soon after this, Lorna Crozier speaks to me:
> "A shadow ripples across her face,
> something between her body
> and the sun. 'You can't get me,'
> she wants to whisper. 'I'm dead.' "

I am not dead, not yet, and I refuse to play dead while alive. Let the shadows do their rippling worst. They can't get me.

✳   ✳   ✳

In 1972 Eric Andersen sang the laments of *Blue River* and I played it over and over, where I lived and in my head, and then I went away. Rene moved to Vancouver. I couldn't stand to be alone so I worked strange long hours, drank in Halifax bars on the nights I wasn't working and invited people to stay at my South Park single rented room. Eric Andersen sang his blue songs for me in that room, many times. Today on Stage 3 I hear him again, an older voice, and I'm as moved as I was over twenty-five years ago, for some of the same reasons and for some different ones, too. Rene and I decided then, those years ago, to try to once again be generous with each other. We moved together to Labrador, then to Manitoba, where we were joined by Sarah and Jan, and where we learned to visit the Folk Festival. I think as I listen to Eric Andersen that they would like his performance, if they could deal with their sadness, and with his.

Sarah and Jan, the fine reality of them, have made the connection between me and Rene worthwhile. We did something very right. I wish that Rene, Jan and Sarah felt the same way, but that too is for them to sort out. I've got my own further movement to find, and memories to make up.

The person who is hosting the small-stage workshop is crying when Andersen finishes "Blue River." She says she hasn't heard the song in a long time and thanks him, straight from her heart – you can hear it. He nods, also moved, and he does not appear to be surprised. He knows. That's why he wrote and sang the words.

\* \* \*

Ben and I go to another workshop, later, on Stage 3, that has J.P. Cormier from Cape Breton and Inconnu from the Yukon, together. The differing styles and content play off each other, with respect and humour. There is enough room to sit near the stage, and there's a breeze to take an edge off the sun. J.P. Cormier reminds me so much of home, and I'm again shown that you really *must* go home again, over and over. There's no choice.

\* \* \*

By the end of the day I'm sun-bent, people-thick, sound-full, and content. There is a mix of music and Crozier in my head, and I don't want to separate them. She finally says, with her words looking me right in the mind's eye,

  "Everything was loud –
  sound and echo inseparable.
  They met where I hung suspended."

 Ben and I leave early to have a shared meal at the Spicy Noodle House or the Bangkok Thai. We'll decide on our way in or later on a shared whim. We move quickly through the Festival's parking lot, laughing as we outrun the mosquitoes, most of them.

*Bird's Hill Park, Manitoba*

# *The Worst Fate*

*T*he worst fate is to be a fan.

On January 19, 2002, a piece by Jeff Blair in *The Globe And Mail* gives details of the diagnosis and prognosis for the Montreal Expos Baseball Club, and it is grim. The diagnosis is terminal apathy and the prognosis is for an inevitably fatal outcome, a year to live, maybe more and maybe less. At the end of this upcoming season, the Expos will either be folded or moved, depending on the dithering commissioner's whim of the day. Major League Baseball is looking for a terminal-care specialist, to make sure the Expos' young and talented players (it is an excellent team; skill has nothing to do with impending death) aren't plundered or abandoned. Jeff Blair, whose intelligent, detailed and occasionally scathingly ironic style is not always perfectly suited to the rah-rah-gee-whiz and/or greed and egocentric foundations of so many sports stories, has the perfect measure of this one. He asks, "Does anyone care?" and then answers his own question by noting the barely stifled yawn of a city and a country. There are a few who care, but nowhere near enough of us. Neither Montreal nor Canada deserves the Expos, and we haven't for a long time.

I lean back into my wicker seat in Timbers Restaurant at the Valhalla Inn on this emotionally and physically cold Saturday morning in Thunder Bay, Ontario, watching the non-smoking side fill for late-breakfast and early-lunch while the smoking side of the room stays empty, and I think about the fate of fans.

A nurse in the Kitikmeot Region of the central Arctic used to periodically declare herself in need of a break from the hurly damn burly of Cambridge Bay. Also in need of some unqualified support, she would easily maneuver her way into an excuse for a paid trip to Yellowknife, saying, "I'm going to see my fans." Sitting in the clean-air side of Timbers Restaurant, waiting for my cell phone to ring, I decide to go see my fans, any of those few memory-brigade supporters who allow unqualified affection. My phone rings and I hit the *talk* button, saying, "Hello, telephone."

\* \* \*

My Air Canada 737 flight leaves Thunder Bay and angles toward Toronto. I've been doing this angling out of places for almost thirty years, from Nova Scotia, Labrador, Norway House, Toronto, Winnipeg, Cambridge Bay, and northwestern Ontario. I watch the frozen lakes and contrasting woods ease away under the plane's right wing, and try to make sense of over-riding passion. Why would anyone care for anything that much, and especially *why* for a men-only team of mostly spoiled and selfish come-from-away types, playing with wildly fluctuating degrees of intensity at a ritual-soaked, high-reflex and variable-fitness contest which either combines the best qualities of chess and ballet or the worst of checkers and hoofing, depending on the day and the mood of the players? Why, indeed? There is no way to explain the passion of a fan. It is related to falling in love; it just is.

\* \* \*

When I was a kid and my mother was still alive, we would visit Meteghan every summer, on Nova Scotia's French Shore. There were many highlights to these visits: my grandparents, uncles, aunts and cousins, the long beach near the wharf, dulse and dry fish, the huge attic in the old house, the store where they sold comic books with a part of the cover cut off so they were dirt cheap, trying to interpret what my mother's family was saying about us or Dad in the wild mixture of English, French and accents that is Acadian, and watching my uncle George play baseball. My mother was the oldest of eight and George was the youngest. He was a swashbuckler, handsome and funny and smiling, unfailingly kind to anglophone nephews and nieces with absent and prickly fathers, and he played ball with flair. We would go to watch and cheer and to exchange grins from sideline to field, and George was always the star of the game.

\* \* \*

When you are lost in the semantic jungle, especially if it's getting dark and you're feeling vulnerable, turn to the dictionary. If you are so foolish to be out there alone without a fan in sight and in immediate danger from words, and you can't find a dictionary you trust or believe, (knowing from experience that some dictionaries are untrustworthy liars), then you have only one positive choice. That is to do a Samuel J. and create your own conceptual list of explanations. This choice does, however, carry the probability of being rejected as an egotistical fool.

I find early in my walking-forward-while-looking-backwards search for connections between baseball and love and fans, and the related essential link between curiosity and caring, that I must turn to the dictionary. On page 301 of *The Canadian Oxford Dictionary* (1998), (whose cover celebrates itself as "the foremost authority on current Canadian English" *and* "the official dictionary of The Canadian Press" – with credentials such as these there can be no possible doubt or challenge), I find these definitions:

"*fan* – a devotee or admirer of a particular activity, performer, etc. [abbreviation of fanatic]," and

"*fanatic* – 1. a person filled with excessive and often misguided enthusiasm for something. 2. informal: a person who is devoted to a hobby, pastime, sport, etc. ... [French *fanatique* or Latin *fanaticus* from *fanum* temple (originally in religious sense)]"

The world becomes understandable when there is a solid dictionary to hand. (I'm convinced, though, that "etc." should be banned from the language, at least the Canadian version of the language. It's too imprecise, broad and vague beyond any hope of capture. Export "etc." to the Americans; they need all the options they can get.) The key words in these definitions, key for me at least, are "admirer," "excessive," "misguided," and "devoted." It keeps coming back to the eye of the beholder, again and again, dictionary or not. This is damned awkward, wonderfully flexible, and absolutely necessary.

\*   \*   \*

*I*n Pictou, Nova Scotia, in the 1950s and in my pre-teens, we played ball in ordinary unmarked bare fields, using hard rubber balls, but not too hard. We were there to have fun, and that's all. When I moved to Kentville at age twelve, it quickly became painfully obvious that these Valley guys took the game seriously. It was not considered to be acceptable, for example, to drop your glove as you ran after the over-your-head wallop. The situation was different here, even for East Enders.

The West Enders were the cream of the Kentville baseball scene, and if you didn't believe that all you had to do was ask them. I was an East Ender. We got t-shirts with VOLUNTEERS in black letters on the front, as a gift from the local (volunteer) fire department. We worked to carve a proper ballpark from an unused and donated-for-a-while undulating edge of the government's Experimental Farm, where some of our parents worked.

Just behind the backstop was a tree-filled deep ravine, so foul balls straight back were cursed and instantly chased by all hands. Our baseballs had all been stolen from the Kentville Wildcats, the summer collegiate Class D-equivalent, semi-pro team that played in our town every summer until 1959, when the whole league folded. These balls had been stolen at moderate risk and exertion, and so were not to be lost lightly. We chased them, and implicitly blamed the ineptness of the hitter for producing the foul in the first place. We were either too dumb or too lazy to build an over-the-top extension to the backstop. Instead, we chased, and we usually found.

The right field was short, with a wire fence backing on another Experimental Farm field, our own version of Yankee Stadium's short-porch, something we all knew of and none had seen. Left field had no fence but ended just as abruptly in a grass bank that slanted steeply down for ten feet and then levelled off, our reverse version of Boston's Green Monster. Ground rules allowed the left fielder to go down over the bank, if he dared, to make the catch. (Rules are all about balance.)

My recollection of this time is that there were six of us who were the hard-core East Enders, including Russ, Charlie, Neil, Arnold, and Hal, but I may be kidding myself about being a part of this elite group. I know I wanted to be, but delusions do exist.

Russ once hit a high and long fly ball, one of the few times he ever did so, and I turned my back to the plate from my left-field position, running down over the bank and out of sight of all on the field, coming back into view a few seconds later, grinning and holding up the ball in my glove, signifying a catch. One of the best things about the honour system is that it opens up a range of choices. Russ doesn't know to this day if I caught it or not. Doubt and revision are two of the most effective enemies of truth and love, and I'm not about to give in to their sour glare at this late stage. Russ was *out*, and still is, due to my spectacular play, of whatever sort.

\* \* \*

My bedroom in Kentville, in the late 1950s and early 1960s, had a large old tube radio. This had been the entertainment and information centre for the family before we got a TV, and it was now mine. The reception and sound were excellent, and I'd tune it to the Boston Red Sox games all summer, especially at night, lying on my back in the dark, listening to the sounds of Fenway Park and often waking later, in the middle of the night, to turn off the radio.

My mother had been born near Boston, when her parents were working for the winter in the U.S. I knew of the slim number of miles between us and them, here and there, but was just becoming aware of the cultural distance. Kentville's Memorial Park and Boston's Fenway Park weren't many miles apart, but the separation of abilities and access seemed increasingly vast, and was.

\* \* \*

One March break in the early 1960s, still years before the establishment of the Expos or Blue Jays, Charlie and I decided to hitchhike to Florida to watch spring training. It had been a long winter, and we were bored. We scrounged about twenty dollars each and hitched to New Brunswick, sleeping in a men's residence TV lounge at Mount Allison University in Sackville one night, and in a similar lounge at the University of New Brunswick in Fredericton the next. New Brunswickers were reluctant ride-givers, so our progress was pathetically slow. We finally got to the New Brunswick-Maine border, sending a card home from St. Stephen, NB, that said, "We're in Calais, and on our way," oblivious of the mispronunciation of our intended rhyme, (the Americans say "Cal-iss" instead of "Cal-eh"), and of the impending end of our intended trip.

The American border guards turned us back, and none too gently, saying that we didn't have enough money to go anywhere, let alone to Florida. Neither Charlie or I was keen on taking "No" for an answer, then or ever, so we bribed a taxi driver to take our two small bags from St. Stephen across the border to Calais in his trunk, while we waited out of sight for the shift change of border guards. We then approached the border, separately, saying we were going to visit (fictitious) relatives in Maine. I got through easily, but Charlie was less nondescript and apparently fit the report the new guards had received. It must have been a slow 1960s day. I went back to look for Charlie, after about an hour, carrying both bags, and they were waiting for me. Both of us were arrested, fingerprinted and photographed, and I still can't decide if it was for real or just good-ol'-Yankee fun intended to scare the country mice – another mystery fly ball.

Either way, it worked. When they eventually spat us out on the Canadian side of the border, warning us that our descriptions (including the nondescript one) had been sent along the longest damned awkward border in the world, "all the way to Idaho," we acknowledged defeat. We spent the next three days hitch-limping home to Nova Scotia, hoping to sneak in without our absence having been noticed, and hoping to intercept the postcard. Again, defeat on all fronts.

Even in adversity and dismal loss, however, there is serious fun to be had, and perhaps true fans and rejected lovers would benefit from having this homily tattooed on some easily observable body part. As Charlie and I bummed rides home, we found ourselves near a highway motel late one evening, as cross-border rejectees so often do. This one was isolated, with a restaurant we could see from our side-of-the-road hitching spot. I went in to ask about room rates, and found that the single rate was just within our budget limit, but not the double rate. So, I registered, just single me, and then Charlie and I entered the restaurant separately as strangers to have a late minimalist version of supper. The smoothness of our ploy was not enhanced by Charlie's seating himself near to me on the counter stools, under the increasingly suspicious nose of the all-in-one motel owner, cook and counter-waiter, and saying to me, "So, stranger, how's it going? You come here often?"

A week later, I received an envelope from the motel guy, with no note, containing the *two* toothbrushes stranger-Charlie and I had left. The wages of sin include prodigal toothbrushes.

＊　＊　＊

The next summer, Charlie and I initiated Plan B. We hitched to Yarmouth, then took the ferry to Bar Harbor, Maine. We had more money, not a lot but more, and our stories were more polished this time, in one case even having a tinge of truth, as I did have a multiple-times-removed cousin in Massachusetts. This cousin had no clue that I existed, let alone was planning (in my story) to be moving into the spare bedroom for a visit, but no matter, the lie held and we made it to the highways of Maine, on the way to Fenway Park in Boston. We didn't send any postcards this time, rhyming or not, but we did discuss it.

After a couple of hours standing on the outskirts of Bar Harbor watching the daylight vanish, a truck stopped. The driver was going to Boston, and he had a proposal for us. Our getting the ride depended on our accepting the deal. He had a load of flowers on board and had to stop at several towns on a winding non-freeway delivery route from Bar Harbor to Boston. We could earn a ride by helping him lug flowers, or we could wave goodbye as he drove away. I had the feeling he'd made this pitch before, several times. We signed on.

For the next several hours we ferried flowers off the truck, at town after town in Maine and Massachusetts, also stopping for fast food and talking with the driver, who was friendly and paid for our supper. Our contention, mine and Charlie's, was that we were the best-hired help he'd ever had. He allowed that we were worth every penny of our wages.

At about 2 a.m., the driver dropped us off in downtown Boston, and drove away. Charlie and I went into several hotels looking for a room, but they were all charging by the hour, a big-city custom we weren't familiar with, so we just kept wandering the streets, getting tired by now. At about 4 a.m., a police car pulled up beside us. Two cops got out, big and not friendly, asking what we were doing. We guessed that they wouldn't be amused by our free-floating wit, so we played it very straight. "Just the facts, sir," Charlie added, but they either didn't hear him or let it pass. They told us to "get in the car, *now*."

One of the cops was from Cape Breton, and he and his cop-partner had a terse low-voiced discussion outside the car, after we got in the back seat. The Cape Bretoner won, as they usually do. They drove us to the affluent Beacon Hill district, then stopped the car and told us, "Don't move, not anywhere." They went up a walk to a large house on a treed street. It was close to 5 a.m. as they banged on the door of the dark house. The lights came on, the door opened, and voices drifted down to us in the car, words not heard, just a firmness of tone and the cadence of direction being given and reluctantly received. It seemed to be a one-sided conversation with the police doing the talking. They came back to the car, motioned us out, and Cape Breton said, "This is a Boston University frat house, and they have a room for you, cheap, for up to one week. See some games, and don't get killed, ok?" He gave us a pat on our shoulders before they drove off.

There were three frat men standing just inside the door, in t-shirts and boxer shorts, sleepy looking, arms folded, not making pro-longed eye contact, the whole hostile repertoire. Charlie and I were tired and confused and not in the mood to absorb attitude from fra-ternal assholes. Charlie opened with "So, guys, how's it going? What've you got to eat?" and I asked if they had a bellhop for our bags. Two of the frat aces just shook their heads (we seemed to be getting a lot of that) and left us to the other one. He waved us up the broad staircase, pointed at a door and said it was ours for a dollar a day, each, and then he walked away. We went in, finding a large bed-room but one that was being used for storage. There were boxes ev-erywhere, and two beds with no bedclothes. The room was a mess. We decided against asking for room service and instead used our clothes for pillows and some old heavy curtains off the floor for blankets. We were tired and this was adequate, excellent in fact. "Say good-night, Gracie," I said, but Charlie was already asleep.

The frat boys told us later, when they finally allowed themselves to speak with us as if we were members of the same species, that the cops had said that we were two hicks from Canada who were going to get killed if they didn't take us in, and that the cops would make their lives consistently miserable if they didn't do the right thing here. This last part was from the Cape Breton cop, who also threat-ened to drop in over the next week, to check on us. These fraternal brethren became almost friendly during our stay, especially when they found that we loved baseball and even understood the rudi-ments of the game. They eventually gave us blankets and towels, but it was clear they thought we were primitive beyond belief. We didn't argue the point, needing the room.

For the next five days we walked to Fenway Park, seeing the Red Sox play Cleveland and then the Yankees. This was the first time ei-ther one of us had ever been in a big-league park, and we were in awe. On our first day, when we came up out of the chilly concrete walkway and then through the usher-guarded arch into the seats, seeing the field for the first time, we stopped and stared, taking it in, the green and flat and size of the outfield grass and the perfection of the infield. We didn't want to move.

Every day we were at Fenway when the gates opened, watching batting practice, fielding drills, the baselines and batter's box being white-lined, the stands filling. We were intent on hearing the sounds and absorbing the images, taking the scent of the majors, learning everything we could. Charlie and I watched the games in the same way, eyes on the field, not talking much, occasionally pointing and nodding, searching for subtleties, trying to see both the whole field and the individual quirks. It's hard work, being a skilled fan.

It was necessary fun to actually see the stars, Mantle and Berra and Colavito and Yastrzemski, the big names being checkmarks on our lives' achievements lists, although we didn't admit that to each other. The more pure purpose, though, was in seeing levels of skill we had only imagined, the hitting and running and throwing and fielding and pitching, usually done with startling nonchalance. We were again overwhelmed, and we both became very subdued for a couple of days, suddenly aware of the distance between us and them. The Church of Fenway, teaching us a painful and sustaining lesson.

I decided on that trip that there were going to be very few things or people in my life for which I'd tolerate the fate or role of fan, and that baseball was one of the few. For the others, I told myself, I was either going to play for keeps, a full active participant, or I'd walk away. It has been useful, having baseball as a fallback and as a guide.

\*    \*    \*

In 1968, Rene and I drove an aging VW Beetle from Nova Scotia to Vancouver, then down the coast to San Francisco before circling back, leaving the collapsed and then deceased Beetle in Topenish, Washington state. We got home to Halifax by taking a bus to Trail, BC, and hitchhiking the rest of the way, getting across Canada in seven days. We were good.

We'd started this whole trip because we had wanted to see the idea of San Francisco, as it was the '60s and the hippie movie was on screens everywhere. It had come belatedly to our minds and lives, and we wanted to see up close where they had set the scenes and auditioned for the parts. We stayed in Sausalito and drove back and forth across the Golden Gate Bridge to the big city, going to the streets and to Haight-Ashbury, watching.

On one of our trips across the spanning bridge, a car coming toward us had a wheel come off, completely off, and it came bouncing at us while the car made a spray of sparks as it skidded on its axle. The wheel and the car both missed us, but not by much. We were impressed, in much the same way the hippies were impressing us, random sparks flying, beautiful and dangerous.

At my urging, we also went to Candlestick Park, then the home of the Giants. Cops, looking as if they were ready for fully armed international conflict and with a matching level of hostile intensity, aggressively waved us into a parking lot. It was the 1960s and we were in San Francisco and they were cops and we were not.

The person at the ticket booth said, "What the hell is *this*?" in a loud rough voice, when I forgot where I was and gave her a *Canadian* $20 bill. We did have American money with us for just this type of encounter with the quaint and culturally impoverished locals, so no lasting harm was done; no one needed to be shot. It was a close call, however, and the need for increased vigilance was noted, in our outwardly apologetic Canadian manner, which hid our scorn.

We saw the Giants, and I cannot remember who the opponents were. What *was* memorable was seeing Willie Mays play. He was in his final career stretch and had stayed in the game much too long, but late in this particular game he got on first and then scored from there on a routine single. I wasn't quick enough, wasn't skilled enough as a fan on this day, to notice if he had been running on the pitch's delivery, before the single was hit. He didn't hesitate at third, running through the coach's stop sign and scoring easily. I was amazed, having just witnessed a legend reach back to display a vestige, a glimpse of his past greatness. It is difficult, however, to explain the intricate complexity and difficulty of scoring from first on a routine single, and I was just beginning to learn the lesson that some things are actually improved by the absence of words. This is a truth, and a metaphor, that I've been slow to grasp. Baseball and Willie Mays teach in circuitous ways, even for fans, especially for fans.

\* \* \*

*W*hile working in Labrador in the 1970s with the then private Grenfell health-care organization, I would occasionally be asked to go to Montreal to raise money for the cause by talking to a local support group. Wilfred Grenfell was a charismatic colonial physician who started a medical service along the Labrador and northern Newfoundland coasts in the early years of the twentieth century, well before the Canadian government thought to do the same in the Arctic and sub-Arctic of Canada. Grenfell had been a genius at milking the guilt and noblesse oblige reflexes of our obscenely affluent society, and the accompanying exotic aura of Labrador, for all they were worth, and they were worth a lot. This baton was handed on, through convoluted historical routes, to some ideologically diverse bedmates, me for instance. I'd be trotted out on some community-hall stage in Boston or Toronto or Montreal to anecdote-on about the Labrador coast, blue-eyed and earnest and looking like I was about three steps off the ski-doo, and the donations would flow. There were times, I'm ashamed to admit, when I almost enjoyed myself.

There were other times, too. I always tried to manipulate these alms-for-the-poor-Labradoreans jaunts to Montreal to coincide with Expos home stands, my theory being that the gods appreciate balance, or should be given the opportunity to learn to do so. On this spring visit I arrived in Montreal's Dorval Airport from Goose Bay, early enough to go directly to Olympic Stadium, found a scalper willing to take my money in exchange for a good seat, stored my suitcase with a reluctantly helpful Big-O administrative office worker, and got to see most of a game. The Expos were honestly trying to be good at this point, in the late 1970s and 1980s, before baseball's liars and double-crossers and incompetents took over. They had skilled players such as Andre Dawson, Gary Carter, Steve Rogers, Tim Wallach, Tim Raines, Ellis Valentine, Bill Lee (I'm including him in this list because he is smart and funny and has a heart), and Warren Cromartie. People were actually coming to the stadium, to watch and cheer and hope. Olympic Stadium has all the glowing warmth and charm of chilled Styrofoam, but with 40,000 people cheering and the Expos winning, the Ugly-O became damn near homey, certainly not Fenway or even Kentville's Memorial Park, but a welcome place to be, nevertheless.

After the game, I collected my bag from administration's care and went by subway to Westmount, where I'd been billeted in a mansion. The place was huge. It had been put on the real estate market the year before due to a significant family sadness, but was then indignantly yanked off the unforgiving block when the expect-ed millions in asking price weren't forthcoming. I was given a grand suite in what I took to be the old and now uninhabited servants' quarters. There was even a functioning intercom, and I earned a polite-whilst-chilly flicker of a smile when I used it to request hot facial towels and a double single-malt, no ice, water on the side, room temperature. Beggars are not permitted to have expensive tastes or a sense of humour, and I have to admit there is a certain logic and necessary balance to this social contract. The system *is* fragile, and things could so easily get out of hand, in an economic-caste sense, if we aren't careful.

\*   \*   \*

Rocky phoned to Labrador from Nova Scotia to tell me to meet him in Montreal so we could watch the Expos play the Phillies. It was 1981. He flew in from Halifax and I came in from Goose Bay, and we met in the lobby of the Hotel Bonaventure. Our reservation had been "lost," that recurrent and pesky city-hotel tendency to misplace things. After a brief yet pointed discussion we were given the bridal suite, a two-level, grossly opulent, prisoner-of-role atrocity designed to drive couples to an early divorce, (so they would then remarry and need the bridal suite again and again – my parents worked in hotels; I know these things). We settled in quickly, immune to opulent angst, checked-out the room's mini-bar, ignored the mirrors, flipped a coin for the acreage of bridal bed (I lost) and got into our most comfortable baseball-watching clothes.

At this point in their history the Expos were exceptionally good, and they were, therefore, appreciated by the we-only-love-winners Montreal fans. These games with the Phillies meant something, a lot in baseball terms, and the stadium was sure to have over 45,000 people firmly seated. We didn't have tickets, but we also had no fear because the local scalpers were a truly resourceful and altruistic group of entrepreneurs. We quickly got moderately good seats for only a moderately bankrupting fee. Rocky then talked us into even better seats by telling the usher that I had come all the way from Labrador just to see this game, my first in a deprived and blizzard-whipped history, after having personally saved hundreds of lives in the last week. He also added to the bored and openly sceptical usher that as a rich physician I was prepared to make a contribution to his very own Big-O retirement fund. This caught buddy's attention, and he subsequently caught my $20. We moved into better seats, behind first base.

After the game, a night game fuelled by beer and hotdogs and peanuts, we ventured into the crowded bar of the Bonaventure, shy but determined to adapt to the alien big-city ways no matter how painful the price. Several of the Phillies came in soon after we got there. Rocky gave me a nudge and then maneuvered his way into two seats at the bar beside them, quickly getting into a freewheeling, loud and funny exchange with several of the players. They were delighted, with my guess being that this was their first encounter with a Canadian who actually talked and laughed and didn't either hide under his bar stool or start to fight at the first hint of a verbal volley. I watched, from under my bar stool, while they played.

The Phillies won again the next night, too.

\* \* \*

Sarah and Jan were born in 1978, and on several occasions in the early to mid-1980s we travelled between the Maritimes and Edmonton, which was the jumping-off airport to and from our home in the Arctic. Making a halfway stop in Montreal was a natural and kind thing to do, just to give the kids a break from the rigors of travel, and the fact that these stops usually coincided with an Expos home stand was pure coincidence. We would stay at the Chateau Versailles or the Chateau Champlain, go up Mount Royal, ride in the horse-drawn carriages, and try out the restaurants in the vain hope that they would eventually measure up to the gourmet standards of the Maritimes, Labrador and the NWT.

Usually, I would go to the games alone on these Montreal oasis-exploration routines, but a couple of times Jan, Sarah and Rene came with me, at my coaxing. I had (and have) hopes that the attitude of being a ball fan would be contagious for the kids and so figured that if I could make this experience fun, actually enjoyable, they might come back. (They have, and do.)

We'd come to Olympic Stadium in the second or third inning so the small-town-northern-isolated kids wouldn't get spooked by the noisy entering crowd, and then we'd leave in the seventh or eighth, no matter what the score and intensity level of the game so they would avoid the obligatory end-of-game hysterical pushing rush for the exit. Unlike most games I go to, where nothing gets my eyes off the field, when we were there with Jan and Sarah I focused on them, their food, drink and entertainment needs, explaining the rationale of the mascot (try that one for logic and depth sometime), and infrequently offering an explanation about something that had just happened on the field and led to the crowd's roar of approval or dismay, trying to keep it both simple and interesting. It seemed to me, as I evaluated my efforts, that I had failed in customarily spectacular fashion, but as the sports reporter in Kentville, Nova Scotia, used to say during my formative competitive years, "It doesn't matter if you win or lose; it's how you play the game."

When we were at home and I was watching a game on TV, one or the other of my daughters would occasionally snuggle up beside me, ostensibly to watch the game. This was always just one of the kids, either one, and she wouldn't stay for long, only an inning or two in real-world time measure. I've never been an admirer of home-run hitters, preferring the make-contact types, and these father/daughter contact games were perfect, as far as I was concerned.

Years later, when Sarah was going to Ryerson in Toronto, my business trips would sometimes coincide with Blue Jays home games (it is truly amazing how often that happens), and Sarah might come to the game with me, again for the contact. Jan was visiting Sarah one week in summer, coming in from Calgary, when I arrived from Kenora for a routine Ministry of Health meeting. (These meetings were calculated to take no action whatsoever on anything of consequence out of fear of offending any political or related business sensitivities, but I figured what the hell, I owed it to my country to be there.) We three lined up on a hot and humid Toronto Saturday and shared the afternoon, me watching the game and them watching the crowd and talking about their lives, and on a couple of loud-crowd instances surprising me and themselves by asking game-related questions. "*What?*" they said, when I looked surprised at these questions. "You think we haven't learned *anything* about baseball?" Then, they'd look at each other and laugh, adding, "Well, you're *right*! But we have to keep you happy by pretending to be interested, once or twice a game," and then they'd crack up again, a shared sisterly laugh that included me. We were having fun.

A few years later, Sarah was dancing on the *Norwegian Sea* or the *Regal Empress*, I forget which one, cruising from port to port in the Caribbean, and Jan was at school in Calgary. I missed them, every day. I received a letter from Sarah on a routine conflicted Kenora Public Health afternoon. She said she was lonely, marooned on the docked ship in Cozumel, Mexico, and had sat down alone to watch baseball on the ship's TV because the sound had reminded her of me. She said she had found the game to be comforting. I'll remember that game, all my life.

\* \* \*

*F*or the 1970s and much of the 1980s, I was smart enough to stay clear of Canada's self-defined mainstream highways, including the communication variety. For the most part this felt appropriate, protected, but not on the days when the Expos were on national TV or regional (southern Canadian) radio. These were the only times that I felt "remote," "isolated" and "cut off," these being the standard self-congratulatory (and delusional) dismissive curses from those locked in the urban-bliss of our southern cities. There *were* coping mechanisms available, however, as there sometimes are. I called the Expos' office to get their TV broadcast schedule and the list of Canadian radio stations that carried their games. This was at the time when the Expos games were carried on many stations, so I had just increased my options while remaining firmly and happily isolated and remote.

The national TV broadcasts provided the easiest opportunity as all it required was for me to rearrange my portion of the health-care world of Labrador or the Northwest Territories or northern Manitoba to fit the baseball broadcast schedule. If the game were to be televised in the evening, as usually happened, then the nursing station nurses and I agreed that there were to be no planned evening doctor's clinics that day, and emergencies had to be real to involve me, none of the I-think-I-might-be-getting-a-headache variety. My nursing bosses (and there was no question as to who was on first, authority-wise) tolerated all of this with quiet scorn; well, most of them did. Some were less quiet and/or more resourceful and these ones might threaten various and exotic viewing fees. To be fair, however, they rarely collected.

Fortunately for the health of the public and for health-care in general, as my medical contribution was definitely the central pillar holding these two above the waves of disease, the Expos weren't on TV very often in Labrador, the NWT or Norway House, only about once or twice a month, April to September. (They never played in October.) As a result it was an event, a big deal.

What is it about us that forces (and allows) the memory bank to hold such a vivid display capacity for our disappointments? Is there a possibility that we have faulty wiring and are poorly evolved, flawed from the get-go? I want to say "surely, not," fearing the stain and consequences of blasphemy, but the flaming doubt remains; I can't will it away. For example, these losses are carved into my memory; they are permanent:

- I was in Cartwright, Labrador, in the late 1970s and it was a Saturday afternoon with the Expos coming up on TV. I was ready, the nurses had been bribed to leave me alone, Rene, Jan and Sarah were reconciled to a bleak afternoon without access to my joyous presence, the comfortable chair and the TV screen were lined up to avoid glare, and the snacks were within easy reach – the works. It was early in the season, April or May, so the weather in Labrador was still stuck at semi-winter with blowing snow and freezing rain, but I was oblivious, mentally immersed in the intricacies of the game. This wonderful oblivion lasted for all of one inning, *one*, when the screen's image vanished into fuzz. My fanatical telephone calls to the world eventually led to an explanation that the freezing rain had coated the relay tower in Black Tickle, (I'm not making any of this up; I have witnesses), and that was that, finished and done, over and kaput until the ice melted off the tower. I considered fabricating someone's medical emergency so as to get an airplane medevac lift to Goose Bay, but it would have taken too long.

- In Spence Bay, then in the NWT and now in Nunavut with a new-old name in Inuktitut, I was in the wonderfully aged nursing station up on the hill and a game was about to start. Shirley came into the living room, and she was apologetic. This rarely happened so I knew I was in trouble. I was, and so was the eighteen-year-old man who needed to talk, and he needed to talk *now*. His visit overlapped perfectly with the length of the game, and he may have wondered about the intensity of my concentration on his problems. Sarah has told me recently that she likes my method of dealing with adversity, a pain or a poorly placed itch or an otherwise awkward event or emotion, by directly and purposefully focusing on it. Forget the "ignore it" advice, which is nonsense. Instead say, "Now, *that* is interesting, that itch. What makes an itch, anyway? Let's focus on it," and this changes the intrusion of the problem; it changes its very nature. I hope the man's NWT itch went away, for a while at least, because the less meaningful game certainly vanished, all of it.

There are other times, luckily, skillfully, when our capacity for joy surfaces, leading to a balancing appreciation for our species' design potential. For parts of two summers Rene, Jan, Sarah and I stayed at Point Prim, PEI, in a small cottage looking out on the narrow strip of water between Nova Scotia and Prince Edward Island, the Northumberland Strait. The days were hot, the sand was red and therefore not crowded, and the kids were curious and caring. We had a good time. In the evenings, late, when Sare and J were sleeping and I was afraid that a radio would wake them, I'd go out to the car and find a radio station broadcast of a ballgame, bouncing in from somewhere-away in the mysterious way that night-time radio waves do.

Usually, the games I would find would be the Red Sox from Fenway, ricocheting all the way to Point Prim. Rarely, I'd find an Expos game in French, and gradually I learned to gather the details and create a general picture of the game, the atmosphere of presence or absence of tension, frustration and skill. In the dark of the car, while swatting at PEI mosquitoes, I wondered if my francophone Acadian mother would be proud of me, or ashamed of my narrow unilingual state, or both. I enjoyed these radio games, in French, more than most others.

∗    ∗    ∗

One of the things about biases that increases their destructiveness is their sneakiness. For instance, my bias about gender-based fan status snuck up on me; I hadn't even suspected myself of being so dumb. When I met Ben, also known as Benita (to get the name-based gender ducks and drakes in order), I'm ashamed to admit that I suspected her interest in baseball to be merely a go-with-the-friend reflex. I was flattered, but I was also wrong. Ben is a fan, the real thing, and it has little to do with me.

We've shared a large number of games on TV and radio, at her place in Winnipeg and mine in Kenora, and while driving to Calgary and Toronto, and we've also gone together to see games in Toronto, and to Montreal to watch the Expos whip the Yankees in a memorable inter-league game where the visiting Americans sounded as if they outnumbered by ten to one the dead-quiet non-crowd of Montrealers. We've also driven to Minneapolis to see the Jays play the Twins. The Minnesotans swept Toronto three straight, but we got to explore bookstores and sculpture parks, and I got to buy dark-blue baseball shirts for Jan and Sarah, and for myself, ones that said TWINS on the front.

Overturning biases can be a straightforward business, it turns out, if it is unnecessary to fight sneaky with sneaky.

\* \* \*

There's a public health conference in Atlanta, in March of this new and improved millennium, and a couple of us produce a mini-workshop on the purpose and methods of media/Public Health interactions. This conference is a big one with 1,300 people attending, and a tiny few of them come to our workshop. (We are semi-good, only needing to offer small and obviously fictitious bribes in order to get them to stay.) After the conference is over I have an afternoon of time-for-me, welcome solitude, so I go on a tour of Turner Field, the home of baseball's Atlanta Braves.

While I enjoy watching the Braves on TV, as they televise most of their games on a cable channel I get in Kenora and have clever, ironic announcers as well as some articulate, humorous players, I also dislike what I read and see of their owner Ted Turner and his

CNN saga. As a bonus, I despise the Braves' logo and their racist tomahawk-chopping chant. I'm curious how I'll react.

It's a cold, windy day in Atlanta, at 8°C or 40°F, and there is not a huge crowd for this one-hour tour. Twelve of us see it all, from the 150 game-day-only $1 seats, the press-box and TV/radio broadcast booths, on to the luxury suites that go for $200,000 a year for a minimum of five years, and then to the Braves' locker room and their dugout. I'm captivated and again realize that once a fan, always hooked. I ask several questions, still being of the opinion that this may lead to honest answers, even in the land of CNN.

The kid showing us around is on his last tour of the season before he leaves for university in Arizona. (I wonder to myself how much this line will attract in tips. It gets $5 from me.) He has a low-key sarcastic delivery that I enjoy, telling of the players' seating pecking-order in the locker room, the feeding habits of the press, and the personality characteristics of the groundskeepers (nasty, and inclined to shout and bite) who are putting down the infield grass as we are led carefully by them. They are getting ready for opening day in one month. The sun on the infield on this March day is cold, nowhere near ready for the game. We are touring a myth.

The Americans know how to do largesse and hype, that is for absolute sure, and I marvel openly at (and inwardly patronize) the world's biggest Coke bottle, situated on the top deck of the stadium and constructed entirely out of baseball products (balls, bats, cleats) and crushed Coke cans. On the one hand, oh dear oh dear oh dear, and on the other, WOW. My favourite part of the tour comes at field level, somewhere I've never been in the major leagues, not in Montreal or Boston or Toronto or Minneapolis or San Francisco, not once. The twelve of us are led into the Braves' dugout, first base side, and I don't sit down because I'd like to think I wouldn't, if I were a player and not a fan. Instead, I lean on the padded barrier at the front of the sunken dugout, one foot higher than the other, intent and quiet, watching for subtleties, the way Charlie and I would have, if we had played there.

Later, I go through the Braves' museum, on my own and slowly, reading and remembering. My father didn't play ball, but he did observe with skill, and he loved to watch the Milwaukee Braves in the 1950s. The Braves are the oldest continuous franchise in the majors, we are told by our last-day tour guide, having been the Boston Braves for about eighty years, then the Milwaukee Braves for just over a decade, and now in Atlanta for thirty-five years. My father and I watched on TV as the Milwaukee incarnation of Braves beat the favoured Yankees in the 1957 World Series, in seven games. I go from glass case to glass case in the museum, seeing the memorabilia of Hank Aaron and Warren Spahn and Lew Burdette and Eddie Mathews, and remember watching all of them with my father. I think of Sarah sitting alone with a game on TV on a docked ship in Cozumel, as I peer into the glass cases.

As I wander around outside Turner Field, long after the tour has finished and I've exhausted the museum's memory bank, I wonder if I'll visit Montreal to watch the Expos one last time on this upcoming last season, as people have done before in Brooklyn with the departing Dodgers, in New York as the Giants left, in Boston and Milwaukee for the Braves, and on and on. Paul Simon says, "Everything put together, falls apart," and so it should. It will be tempting to go for a last Expos look and also tempting to call Rocky to see if he will join me there. I may, but the odds are against it judging by my track record. I seem to prefer to leave things as they find themselves.

As I walk away from the ballpark I realize that I'm glad that I've restricted my fan status to games, and not for other contests of will. As Rocky would sometimes say, usually with a grin, "I've enjoyed as much of that as I can stand."

The worst fate is never to have been a fan.

*Toronto and Kenora, Ontario*
*Atlanta, Georgia*
*Montreal, Quebec*

# Delusional Sheep Invite a Lion

*J*ack Hildes came to do a talk in St. Anthony, Newfoundland.
This was one of those you-are-hereby-invited-into-the-lions'-
den, we-dare-you invitations. I had heard of Hildes from reading the health portion of the Royal Commission on Labrador, in
which he had not been laudatory regarding the International Grenfell Association, "The Mission" it was still then called on "the coast,"
the Labrador coast. This was in 1974.

St. Anthony was the medical and administrative headquarters of
Grenfell's remote health-care service, and its 200-bed hospital, air-
ambulances and web of administrators offered proud testimony to
Grenfell's seventy-five years of service zeal in a region of huge need.
The hospital was also a shrine and an example of just how far the
tentacles of twentieth century medical hubris had reached. As one
typically autocratic and obnoxious chief-physician-and-god said to a
pediatrician who wanted to refer a critically ill child to St. John's,
rather than have major surgery done in St. Anthony, "I didn't build
this hospital to send kids to St. John's." The pediatrician put the
child's welfare first, right up at the front of the line, and sent her off

to St. John's, on a Friday morning. By Monday he was looking for work, on the mainland.

Jack Hildes was not impressed, seeing the service as primitive, even dangerous, as he judged its foundations to be moralistic, colonialistic, xenophobic, and medically shaky, at best. Hildes did not like Grenfell. He was also the biggest lion around, and he knew it, so he accepted the invitation without hesitation.

Hildes had his own box of hubris. He was not averse to autocratic imposition of his will, and he demanded excellence and nothing less, having decided that skill justified the forgiveness of many sins. He was a Winnipeg-based gastroenterologist turned administrator, a medical specialist who did not believe in basing a remote health-care service on nurse practitioners and lay dispensers and a few family doctors, as did Grenfell.

Instead, in the vaguely similar service he ran in northern Manitoba and a central part of the Keewatin Region of the Northwest Territories, he chose to emphasize recruitment and retention of family doctors and several long-term urban-based specialists in surgery, pediatrics, dentistry and psychiatry. These specialists periodically left their regular city practice to visit the small hospitals in Hodgson, Norway House, Churchill and a related score of communities served by nursing stations. Hildes was not involved with staffing the stations, nor did he want to be. The family doctors he provided for the small hospitals, and for the "fly-in" visits to the stations, had a high turnover, a sad fact which was accepted as being a necessity of the business, a flaw tolerated because it was unavoidable. Specialists, in Hildes' view, were a more advanced state of medical life-form than primary-care people, even if the latter were needed and occasionally noble.

Aboriginal people escaped Hildes' hierarchy. They were separate from it, above it, and he learned from them while acknowledging their different reality. This intrinsic respect was not a historical foundation of Grenfell, who *saved* the Innu, Inuit and Settlers, whether they liked it or not. More and more often, they did not like it.

Jack Hildes, on the 1974 visit, took the offended anger of the St. Anthony hospital crowd and threw it back in their faces with scornful humour, completely at ease, one hand self-tied behind his back just to even-up the odds. His calm disdain was easily readable on his creased face, a lion amongst delusional sheep.

After it was over I approached Hildes, catching up to him as he walked alone in the cathedral-like atmosphere of the hospital entry, accidentally just the two of us in this large round area, as things sometimes set themselves up. I said that I admired his style and would like to work with him someday, preferably soon. He looked me over, openly fed-up with and dismissive of anything and anyone linked to Grenfell, and then curtly advised me to stay working in Labrador, for years, and then to call him again when he'd see what he thought. I considered this, and offered the equally curt opinion that while he should not hold his breath waiting for my call, he *should* get stuffed, and soon. He laughed and walked away. I did, however, take his advice, all of it.

Later, I worked with Hildes for several years, learning to admire his courage and wisdom, and most of all his depth of heart. I was also thankful, and still am, for his limitless supply of anti-sainthood potions. We all have our debts.

*Grand Lake, Labrador*

# The Trains at Banff

*I*t's 6 a.m., and I'm waiting for the coffee to cook in the Hemingway Studio at the Centre for the Arts in Banff, Alberta. That's not Ernest but Peter Hemingway, the architect, who has his name on the plaque by the outside door, and in my scoring system every connection gets points. The "Peter" alone has to push it into the fate category. As Bill Richardson said on CBC radio, as he assisted the world on its drive through Saskatchewan a thousand kilometres ago, "Do *not* ignore the signs," and he had his truthful tongue well away from his cheek. I won't ignore the signs, and there are many.

\* \* \*

Rene and I drove into Banff in a VW bug in the summer of 1968, on our way to San Francisco to see the hippies and to look for connections. Neither of us had ever seen prairie or mountain, and we were wide-eyed and awestruck as we chugged across the country in that black bug. (Why do insects have such short futile lives, instead of our species' lengthy profound meander? Why do they tolerate such a situation?)

In Calgary, at a stoplight, someone spotted our Nova Scotia plates and our backseat piled to the roof with camping gear, and they honked, waved, smiled. We took it to be friendly, totally.

Driving into the mountains for the first time, over thirty years ago, was overwhelming. We found a place to stay at Banff and then wandered the streets, liking the feel of the air and the backdrop of the mountains.

Thirty-four years later, at 6:15 a.m. in the round Hemingway Studio on the side of a mountain, the coffee is ready, but I'm not. The furnace blowing hot makes the air swirl and my few early morning candles flicker. Through the window and the mesh of tall straight spruce and fir I can see the beginning of daylight, and I listen for the Banff train whistle to call. I'm in need of that orthodox sound, of the reassurance of tradition, because I'm in the midst of challenging a taboo. This one reads, or so it reads to me, that one must not relate with gratitude, respect and affection to those who are no longer friends-of-your-heart, the departed partners, lovers, spouses and friends, those who are no longer connected. While there are episodic field reports of eccentric exceptions, more often we hear the loss of name and the use of "my ex," and we measure scorn, anger and ill-will where there once was companionship. I'd like to acknowledge those who have shared caring, even for those with bitter baggage, and even to myself.

Paul Simon sang of trains blowing the direction when he said, "Everybody loves the sound of a train in the distance; everybody thinks it's true." We have our own trains in the distance, arriving and leaving, and we all think they are true.

\*  \*  \*

Banff is a place I've wandered through many times, and it has metamorphosed from small to crowded and from low-cost and comfortable to rich and pushy. It's not the only place with such afflictions, not by any means. Have you wandered around Ganges on Salt Spring Island lately, in August? Or Cavendish strip, PEI, or Chester, Nova Scotia, or Granville Island Market in Vancouver on a Saturday, or Toronto Island on a hot Sunday afternoon, or Kenora on any sunny day in July? It helps if you try to see through the gaudy falseness to the centre of the place, the true sound in the approximate distance. As Jan said, after we parked the car and sauntered our way to a Banff restaurant at 9 p.m. on a cold and uncrowded March evening, "I *like* this place; the tourists aren't so bad when they're not here."

* * *

When the kids were five we visited the Banff Springs Hotel, and they liked to dress up for the dining room. The Japanese tourists were fascinated by their twin-ness combined with their calm dining-room style, and asked to take pictures. They didn't exhibit enough shyness in making this intrusive request, not to suit my reserved Maritime taste, but we let it happen. The pictures were taken, and are either long-gone discarded, or are in some photo albums in Japan, experiencing the preservation of strangers' images, never changing.

We had lived north for all of the kids' lives to that point, in Labrador and the Northwest Territories, so other than for brief summer visits to Nova Scotia and PEI they hadn't had a chance to play in water. They didn't know how to swim so hotel swimming pools took on a lure, a challenge.

In the outdoor Banff Springs Hotel swimming pool one warm July evening, Jan and I were playing around in one part of the shallow end, with Rene and Sarah over to the other side of the large pool. The pool was crowded with parents and kids, and with a group of adult tourists. The balcony overlooking the pool was lined with casual watchers, leaning on the railing, relaxing with the evening. In the midst of the background murmur and splashing flow of sounds I heard a loud, happy, proud voice say, "Pete, look, *LOOK*! I can swim, I can *SWIM*!" Sarah had on two small water wings at her upper arms, and she had moved away from Rene, over her head in water depth, and she was on her own, swimming. The beams on the faces of so many people turning toward her were powerful, showing our species' pride in its own for one shared instant, but Sarah was oblivious to them. She was not oblivious to me and us, nor to her ability to learn and to exert her will and move past failure. I often think of that moment in Banff when I share time with Sarah, now an adult and still consistently moving toward the deep end, still swimming.

*   *   *

A bunch of us health-care types were at a meeting in Red Deer, Alberta, on the day fourteen women were killed in Montreal. It was obvious that *all* of us loved women, and had daughters and sisters and women friends. It seemed that all of us were hurt more than we could say, perhaps more than we could feel. There are things I remember about the next few days:

- I read of the Montreal policeman, a father, who found his daughter dead at the school. Thinking of Jan and Sarah, I couldn't bring myself to imagine being able to cope with that. Years later, one of my daughters was told by a performance instructor that the way to cry in a scene, on cue, was to imagine, or remember, the very worst thing in your life. She wouldn't tell the students what she herself used, and I agreed with her reticence and felt sorry for everyone who has to cry on cue, who has to imagine that depth of pain.

- A friendly acquaintance, a woman, told me that I could not possibly feel what women were feeling after the killings, and in fact, my maleness was just

45

another part of the problem that killed these women and so many more. I knew what she meant, and could not decide who I despised more following her understandable and silly brutality, me or her. I still haven't decided.

• Another woman friend, at the Red Deer meeting, agreed with me that escape might be therapeutic. At the end of one day's work we rented a car and left, driving to Rocky Mountain House and then on to Banff, where we had a late dinner at the Hotel. The dining room was full and very busy. We were quiet, relaxed but quiet. We got back to Red Deer at about 2 a.m., alive, coping. We did not escape, however, not ever.

I don't remember my presentation from that meeting; it was less than peripheral.

\* \* \*

On one of our family trips to Banff, when the kids were at starting-school age, we took the cable car up Sulphur Mountain. I am not fond of heights, and Bob Hope's line about getting dizzy on a thick rug has always seemed too true to be funny. Sarah and Jan are aware of several of my neurotic twitches, including the aversion to heights. On the Banff cable car, they spontaneously positioned themselves closely on either side of me, talking about anything they could think of, to distract me. I was moved by their affection and generosity, as I knew at least one, and maybe both, also didn't enjoy potential-free-fall heights. (Some coincidences are relative.) Their ploy was effective, as I *was* distracted. I admire my daughters; they've been fine role models.

\* \* \*

*O*ne recent year, I was able to talk Benita into taking the marathon bus trip from Winnipeg to Vancouver and back, thirty-two hours each way, in December, nothing but highway and bus-stop restaurants and small town freight-stops at 2 a.m. in eastern Saskatchewan. Actually, I didn't so much *talk* Ben into the trip, it was more that I bribed, harangued and groveled my way to victory – whatever works. She was surprised that the trip "out" to BC was almost bearable, uncomfortable and sleepless, yes, bad food and grim washrooms, oh yes indeed, but there were many more worthwhile views and free-theatre glimpses into people's lives than she had expected. "I just *so* told you so," I said, grammatically flawed but nevertheless never one to let a gloating opportunity rumble on by. However, I did agree, after only a token and minimalist splutter of protest, to stop for an overnight rest at Banff on the way back. What the hell, I'm just here to serve.

The return bus from Vancouver got into Banff at about 4 a.m., to cold and empty streets. Not only the tourists were locked up tight and warm and secure; everybody was. We felt alien and free, cold and elated, as we walked from the bus station to the nearest hotel.

I continue to find it odd that we remember some things so completely, with feeling and texture, while others are just stirred into the stew of mixed-up almost-gone memories. This 4 a.m. walk in the winter mid-night freeze along Banff's back-street, for example, is tattooed on the front of my recall, like a signpost or a meaningful event, and I don't know why. (I can guess, but it's only that, a made-up shot-in-the-4-a.m.-dark. Sometimes, a train is shaped like a bus. It's strange, but it happens.)

\*   \*   \*

When Jan moved to Calgary to study contemporary dance, it gave us a chance to share Banff, several times. When I drove her out to start classes in September, or visited for her performances, or because one or both of us had been struck by loneliness and requested a visit, we often went to Banff, sometimes just for the day. We share it well.

The University of Calgary has one big dance production each year in March, called Main Stage. Even though Jan insists that I should *not* count on her being in this, as it's by audition, I *do* count on it, as I've seen her dance. She's a lock, but I am careful to not mention this opinion to J-person, as it has the potential to stretch the elastic father/daughter bonds, possibly to the point of snapping back to zap the father. What I did do, however, on one occasion, as soon as I knew the dates, was to call the Banff Centre and ask about the process of applying for the writers' residencies I had heard about.

I'm only good in this type of informational gathering exercise if the other person is themselves good – friendly, not too literal regarding terms, not putting me on terminal-hold to answer other much more interesting and important calls, or (as I suspect) to go get a double de-caff no-fat no-foam latte while I wait. No, I'm definitely not good in that situation, tending toward being borderline impatient and slightly irritable, sometimes even moderately early in the exchange, at about the five-second mark. I share this introspective revelation because it was irrelevant in my exchange with The Centre at Banff, proving that I *can* raise my game, given the inclination. I have to work on the inclination.

On this occasion, it took a few phone transfers, and answering-machines that got me punching 0 to get back to the live person and dealing with queries of "*What* do you want to find out about?" and "*Who* are you wanting to speak with?", before we understood each other. I came to understand that Banff Centre has a group of buildings called the Leighton Studios, for writers, painters and musicians, and that one of the aforementioned creative types can apply for a "self-directed residency" at these, but (here it comes, I thought, we're finally going to get to the *But*-point) a self-defined creative person has to be judged suitable before being accepted. The word "adjudicated" was used.

"Adjudicated?" I said. "Did you say '*adjudicated*'? What in hell is *that*?"

"It is this," she said, her tone the epitome of patience. "You send us samples of your previous work, and outlines of what you plan to be working on, and names of three people we can call for reference, for example a publisher. Then, we sift through the applications to see how you stack up. Judging by this conversation, I'm looking forward to assessing your application." (I got in.)

\* \* \*

For the week I spent in the Leighton Studios Artists' Colony, I'd get up at about 6 a.m. in the separate residence where I slept, then shower, dress and go out in the dark along the snowy path to the circular Hemingway Studio. I'd get the coffee going, with the radio on CBC for that opening time, and then watch the night ease to light, with the curved wall of pane-windows changing from closed-in reflectiveness to a view of a treed slope. Early one morning, several elk wandered calmly and slowly by the wall of windows, oblivious to my watching.

I wrote every day from about 6:30 or 7 a.m. to 3:30 or 4 p.m., and then walked downtown, to the bookstore and grocery store and Coyotes restaurant. For three of the evenings, I drove into Calgary to watch Jan dance, and to applaud. I then drove back to Banff, getting in well after midnight, but already enough habituated to the routine to find it easy facing getting up at 6:30 a.m.

Jan came out for a couple of days, after her performances were over, and she read and recuperated while I wrote. In the front of a book called *The Writer's Desk* by Jill Krementz, which J gave me, I've taped a picture of me sitting at the shelf-desk in front of that wall of windows in the Hemingway Studio. Jan took the picture, and I appear to be relatively relaxed.

\* \* \*

We were having breakfast at Coyotes one morning, Jan and I, when we saw a young woman sitting on a bench across the street. She was in her late teens or early twenties, and she looked tired and dejected. I thought that she looked hungry, too, but have no idea why I thought that. We discussed how one of us could approach her to ask if she needed a breakfast, but she was too quick or we were too slow; she left. Sometimes, we agreed, it is difficult to rise to the moment before you've had your coffee. Both of us felt that we blew it, and we were not sure if we'll do better next time.

∗    ∗    ∗

Late one evening, I'm on a writer's roll and am trying to keep up with the words flowing from the stolen Delta Hotels ballpoint pen. (Later, the editor-who'll-I'll-then-be will clear-cut this output down to only a few lines, but that knowledge of the probable future doesn't dim the rush of going full-tilt at in the candle-lit desk in Banff's Colony.) Later still, at around midnight, I walk from the hillside Centre, down the hill, and around the town's streets. It's cold out, and I'm good for it, and so are a bunch of other folk, some of them utilizing brother alcohol's pseudo-warming effects. We wave and weave, and avoid any hassle. I hear a train going through, blowing and not stopping. I walk toward the sound of train wheels and heaviness, but don't get to it before it's gone. I turn around and start back up the hill, toward my home-for-a-while. I'm feeling finally that I know the truth about trains, and it is just fine, that truth. It is acceptable.

*Banff, Alberta*

# *Moving Glass*

---

*I*t's eleven on a Saturday morning near the end of February and I'm alone except for Jacob the dog. We are walking out on the ice of Populus Lake, and I've got a plastic pail and ladle in one hand and a shovel in the other. Populus Lake is in the middle of northwestern Ontario, and it's taken me a while to get here. I have some adjusting to do so I can go on to the next place. It seems that I am suspended. I stop to turn around, to listen and to look back at the little cabin sitting on the rise of a point of land. Jacob looks up at me, waiting, puzzled, and then hoists a canine shrug and takes off back into the woods, gone. I listen.

This lake is hill-locked, reached by a forty-kilometre twisting trail on ski-doo northeast from the Highwind Lake road where we left the truck, just off the highway to Sioux Narrows, south of Kenora. The only sounds I can hear are crows, as if from a long distance, and a closer and smaller bird, maybe a Whiskey Jack.

Lyle and Bill left earlier on their ski-doos to check traps and randomly explore while I stayed at the cabin to do the dishes, have a stand-up basin bath, sweep the floor, and now to refill the five-gallon water pail from a bore-hole in the half-metre-thick ice, about one hundred metres out from the shore edge. It's warm today at about -10°C, with low clouds, no wind, and a comfortable dusting of snow.

I continue to look back at the cabin, seeing the thick gray smoke coming from the chimney, far too thick as the damper is closed-down on this warm morning. Sometimes there's not a lot of choice. I remember the cabin at Grand Lake, Labrador, and try to figure out how a person can move on or learn how to stop preventing that from happening.

✳ ✳ ✳

Rene and I moved to Labrador in 1973, and I soon became obsessed with the idea of building a cabin near water, with a view. Labrador had caught me by the mind and introduced me, belatedly, to the concept of place. I hadn't been listening to place before Labrador. Then Rene joined the idea and we were off. We read books, many of them, and talked with older Labrador people about cabins they had built, all the way from small trapper's "tilts" to large multi-room homes. We took notes and shared the planning.

One Christmas we chartered a four-seater single-engine Cessna, which landed on skis on a narrow river just off the end of Grand Lake so we could spend Christmas in a neighbour's cabin, Harold's place. We stood by our pile of things as the Cessna took off, after the pilot had confirmed that he'd be back in a week to pick us up. "Don't forget," he said. We were sixty kilometres from North West River with no way to reach anyone, no phone or CB radio. The lake wasn't yet frozen so there was no walking option either. We were there, and that was that.

It was a safe week, with a warm woodstove in the cabin and piles of dry driftwood along the nearby lake edge. We had a Christmas tree and presents and a wonderful chance to really *look* at someone's hand-built cabin. We visually and verbally took the place apart, log by log, door by windows by wood box by stove by bed. We went to school in Harold's place near the mouth of the Beaver River at the west end of Grand Lake; we learned what we could.

Over the next three years, we built our own cabin in a shallow rock-filled scoop of a cove about half-way along the north side of Grand Lake, opposite Cape Caribou. This cabin was started in the summer, when the blackflies were so thick that Rene's red shirt looked black, all of it, one humid and still August morning.

It took us hours to go back and forth on summer and fall week-ends and evenings, about forty-five minutes each way, in our green Hudson Bay freighter canoe with a 9½ HP motor on the flat back.

The work was also done in winter, getting there on ski-doo and towing a komatik, watching for bad lake ice, and for fragile shelf-ice at the Narrows between Little and Grand Lakes, and cursing the middle-of-the-lake slush that bogged us down, time after time. We did it sometimes as just-we-two and sometimes with friends, Janet and Antony, Norman and Madeline, and we even had visits from Rene's father Rocky and my brother Mark. The logs used were ones we could chop, saw, peel, and carry ourselves without using any power tools, not ever.

Rene built the windows, after getting the glass panes there by boat, carefully wrapped and lap-held, and those two windows looked south and west over the lake toward Cape Caribou and to-ward where Harold's Christmas cabin was, thirty kilometres away. We built the cabin roof, which seemed much larger than the 3-metre by 5-metre cabin floor, and also the heavy double-planked door and the log-legged table and the bed-platform. The outhouse was placed along a path well back from the water and was decorated with tacked-up photos and enhanced by scented candles. We used a Sty-rofoam seat kept in the cabin for warmth and then lugged under an arm along the wet or snowy or fly-thick path. It became a comfort-able walk.

Our stove was a small cast-iron reject from Sheshatshiu which wouldn't stay alive and hot for longer than four hours, so mornings were cold and required quick leaps into clothing and to the stove with kindling and logs and pleading – my job. Rene's matching job was to master the cooking potential of the stove, and she did this with skillful ease, making meals and baking bread and desserts. We ate well. We lived well at the Grand Lake cabin, for a year, and then we left.

✳   ✳   ✳

*L*yle and Bill asked if I wanted to join them for a weekend at Lyle's trapline cabin, deep inland east of the Lake of the Woods. I did and dug around in my Kenora apartment to find my big Arctic boots, the ripped-and-wearable snow pants given to me by Sister Eunice, my sun-bleached beaver-flap hat, the thick ski-doo gauntlets, and the parka Rene got for me in Ottawa in 1975 or 1980, I can't remember which. They all still fit. I also took care to have my new, warm wool socks with me, a combined Hanukkah and Christmas gift from Ben.

The route to Lyle's cabin first took us to Highwind Lake Road, with a ski-doo, food boxes and gas in the back of the pickup truck and another ski-doo plus sleds in the open trailer we were towing. After we stopped and parked the truck we hooked up the sleds then loaded and lashed down the contents. There was a sense of ritual recall, an echo. We adjusted our clothes to fit the sun and -15°C temperature, and I then perched behind Bill on the older and stronger of the machines. It was almost noon and we were gone, out of reach on the land, the first time in fifteen years for me.

We went over frozen lakes in soft and shallow snow, perfect going in a bright sun and not-too-cold temperature. The lakes are named Ethelma, Hillock, Dryberry and Betula. There are long stretches of narrow trails either in-between or beside these lakes, skirting which might be either thin ice or thick slush. The overland portions were often narrow, through kilometres of evergreens, poplars and alders, twisting and angling over and over, dodging branches, not going too fast but fast enough not to get bogged-down. Lyle

54

and Bill were good at this so I just held on, trying to control my musing and metaphor-seeking inclinations so I could be alert enough to avoid the branch to the face (another metaphor) and just watch the world flow by, so that it surrounded us.

There is a particular type of moment that occurs in very narrow trails, ones with alder and poplar branches jutting out low and often into the faces of the ski-doo riders. As I looked ahead over Bill's shoulder, I was watching the trail and moving my head out of the way of these low branches. Every so often we would approach a clump of branches, a thicket with no option of dodging except to bend over, head down behind Bill's back, feeling the branches whip across my shoulders and bent helmet. The moment I both feared and enjoyed came as I raised my head, bringing it back up from the bent-neck huddle behind Bill, as there was a second of vulnerability when I may be looking up just in time to see a branch smack me in the face. I got so I could guess from Bill's shoulders whether or not we were about to get hit again, but that necessarily blind transition from past to present still retained a quick rush of risk. These moments have an element of enjoyment if you survive them, and I wouldn't eliminate any, even if I could.

Soon after we pulled out of this tunnel of trail Lyle pointed to the land, the shoreline, and we pulled in to a small rock cliff, a rocky point of land. There was a low beige area of flat rock face extending up from the lake snow about one metre high and three metres wide, and it was sheltered by a quarter metre of rock overhang. On the beige surface there were pictographs in red paint, faded but still clear and definite. Someone had stopped here to paint, long ago. There were several stick figures connected to geometric designs. Two child-size handprints were also there, fingers and palm and thumb, the whole small hand. I stood staring at these drawings, especially the hands, trying to connect to several angles of time, trying to be there and here.

I have read about pictographs and pictograms and can never remember which is which, paint on rock or images carved into rock. I do remember that many think the drawings were done by shamans and convey messages through common visionary symbols, all those geometric configurations coming to peripheral people with migraines and/or supernatural visitations, or to those who choose to press down on their closed eyelids. As I stood looking at these red drawings I recalled the role of rock-based minerals in preserving the art for hundreds of years and the fact that aboriginal rock-art is similar and related, from many completely disconnected parts of the world. The illusion of race and distance leaps into the foreground of pictographs, as does the silliness of defining the origin of art's motivation.

The feeling I wanted to have was that these were just-for-the-fun-of-it Anishinaabe art work painted from a canoe on a warm and calm early summer day, but then I caught myself and asked (not aloud) what in hell do I know about artistic motivation anyway, especially that of the Anishinaabe who followed the retreating glacier? Nothing is what I know, but I was determined to hold on to the projected feeling of ease anyway because I was having fun, right here on the same lake by the same beige and sheltered chunk of rock.

My favourite image from this blind-in-the-sun visit back to the day these pictographs were painted centuries ago was that of a nine-year-old girl, dipping her hand in the paint and making prints, and they caught, they lasted. I took off my ski-doo mitt and knelt in the snow so I could put my own hand on the painted print, gently, a father saying hello to this other long-gone child and to my own now-grown daughters.

Then we got on the ski-doos and followed the small mid-lake marker shrubs of Dryberry Lake, placed here a few weeks ago by Lyle so he wouldn't wander onto thin ice in a snowstorm. We went from lake to lake, through trails and over marshes, and at one point I stayed with the machines while Lyle and Bill walked into the woods by a small frozen stream to check traps. I sat in the sun on the warm and quiet ski-doo, listening to the old lake as it slowly recovered from our new noise.

After another hour or two (time collapses and expands) we got onto Populus Lake, and at the very bottom we pulled up the short steep point of land to Lyle's 3-metre by 4-metre cabin, backed by Sandridge Hill as shown on Lyle's trapline map #KE 118, which we'd occasionally looked at during our stops. We drove up to the cabin almost nonchalantly, after three twisting hours.

✳ ✳ ✳

Rene and I shared trips like this on ski-doo, over and over, from North West River to Grand Lake or out on Lake Melville toward Butter and Snow and then to The Islands and once or twice across Lake Melville to the base of the Mealy Mountains. We also went from Nain to Davis Inlet, from Cartwright to Paradise River and Separation Point, and most often just up the hill at Cartwright toward Burdette's Pond, to watch and listen to the town and to get some dry spruce for the fireplace. We never did this together in the Kitikmeot Region of the Arctic so it's almost twenty years ago, making me wonder why some lost things stay so connected.

In the middle of a particularly tortuous stretch of cut-trail just before Dryberry Lake I missed the past and shared times so deeply that I could neither remember how I got to be here or where I'm going next.

✳ ✳ ✳

In the evening after we unloaded the sleds, allowed the stove to heat the cabin and had some supper, Bill was outside in the dark. He called for us to come out, to look. What we saw was a sky full of stars, with no light pollution to dim our sight, none. The last time I experienced this privileged view was in 1985 in Bay Chimo, NWT. This Ontario time, the three of us stood on the point and tried to cope with the height and density of the sky. Then we went back inside to the warmth and drinks and stories.

The trick is to be able to link the two, cabin and sky, without losing either one, or yourself. The same can be said, I am discovering, for past and present. Link the two, but do it so as not to lose all of either or all of yourself.

In the morning Lyle and Bill asked if I wanted to come with them to check traps, and both seemed remarkably nonplussed when I said that I wanted to stay home, clean up, and perch on a birch-stump neatly balanced on an overturned bucket so I could write.

I had thought that I might be able to steal some time of my own on this trip, as is often done in airports and hotel rooms, and so had brought a pen and coil-bound scribbler, for notes on the outline of a piece on ski-doo trips and cabins. I had been prepared for a nostalgic heart-tug connected to the travelling and being in a lake-edge cabin but was then blindsided by the actual force of the memories. It's unusual for my emotions to sneak up on me (that's my self image), so I had broken one of my own rules of inner life, I must have. I didn't know which one, not yet.

I had also broken another rule, so it was turning out to be a weekend of progress for the discarding of self-inflicted rules. This second one avoids word-paralysis and was also learned the hard way. It tells me to not bring a book by an author whose writing I bow to, not on any trip where I plan to write, especially if my directions are unclear or conflicted. This eliminates many authors from my suitcase. (When I asked Lyle about having a dog on a trap-line, he said it's only a problem if you want to stay hidden. A strong-willed and strong-scented dog is not a problem if you're out in the open for all to see, including the ones you're hunting.)

On this trip I had been careless and had brought Barry Lopez's *Winter Count*. When I found that I was going to have time to write, I buried Lopez in the far bottom of my shiny waterproof sports bag. Before Barry bit the blue bag I allowed myself a glance at the quotes he'd put at the beginning, the thematic signposts. I wasn't going to read about his trip, not yet and not here, but what harm could come from a quick look at his vehicle's license plate? Lopez displayed three passages. One was from William Pitt Root, no date or site or source given and I'd never heard of him:

"After the long letters
have been written, read,
abandoned, after
distances grow absolute
and speech, too,
is distance, only
listening is left."

The second one, on the same page as W.P. Root, was from Jorge Luis Borges, and I couldn't remember which book, nor were we told:

"We are ignorant of the meaning of the dragon in the same way that we are ignorant of the meaning of the universe, but there is something in the dragon's image that fits man's imagination, and this accounts for the dragon's appearance in different places and periods."

On the directly opposite page, in italics and without attribution so presumably by Lopez himself, was the following passage:

"Among several tribes on the northern plains, the passage of time from one summer to the next was marked by noting a single memorable event. The sequence of such memories, recorded pictographically on a buffalo robe or spoken aloud, was called a winter count. Several winter counts might be in progress at any one time in the same tribe, each differing according to the personality of its keeper."

That'll teach me to break my own rules, to dig my own traps. I covered *Winter Count* with as much of my excess winter clothing as I could find. Symbolism is everything, almost.

✳ ✳ ✳

Jacob comes running back out of the trees, apparently pleased that I'm no longer stalled. He's now intent on interfering with my progress as I trudge along the lake carrying a water-full bucket and a shovel. I like Jacob. He doesn't seem to be overburdened with introspection and subsequent self-doubt but instead just gets on with it, at least until whatever it is becomes awkward or he loses interest.

As I plod up the steep incline to the cabin, I plan to open the damper a bit – heat or no heat, that thick smoke is not acceptable. For the first time in years I wonder about the possibility of having a small cabin of my own, on Grand Manan or PEI or in the Gulf Islands, for example, or maybe on Populus Lake. Sharing such a cabin would also be a possibility. I am leading into further movement.

Jacob barks at something, repeatedly and sharply, but I don't see anything except a new stir of breeze giving sound to the now-moving trees. I say, "It's just the trees, Jacob," and he looks at me, not convinced, or maybe he wants to deal with his troubles in his own way. The breeze does drop abruptly, I notice, and the trees do stop their swaying creak. "Well done, Jacob," I say, and then go into the empty cabin to put the water away and sweep the floor again and to speak gently to some distant echoes before I listen, more carefully this time.

*Populus Lake, Ontario*

# *Navigating Patterns*

*I*'m navigating the past, circling back for another look. Intent *is* important, not as central as we'd have it, but important never theless, and this is intended to be a navigation of the past, not a negotiation, and by no means a negation. We all dig our own traps, and that part is unavoidable, but what is possible is to choose *why* we will dig, and where, and what implement we'll use. There has been some friendly help for me in this circling back. The sources and extent of this help have been different than I expected, and from only a few of the expected sources, a liberating surprise.

✳   ✳   ✳

On the wall of my Kenora apartment I've got a rug weaving done years ago by Maudie Keefe of Black Tickle, Labrador. It is intricate and beautiful, and was a gift from someone who was a nurse and a friend. The wall-rug has a complicated angular pattern, thick with rich colour, made by weaving leftover bits of sock-wool into a burlap potato sack. I once asked Maudie about the pattern, and she just shrugged, the way diviners of patterns sometimes do, oblivious or protective of origins and possibly quietly scornful of my need to ask. If you don't know, I can't tell you.

∗   ∗   ∗

It is January in Kenora, cold sun on sharp wind on quiet life, blowing along on its way. I watch a raven dip and rise, playing tag with the wind, over the narrows and winter walking-bridge between Kenora's mainland and Coney Island.

I've been given a tape of *The Morningside Years* by my daughter Sarah, a thoughtful gift from a Christmas Eve visit by Sarah and Jan. I've saved the tape, waiting, and now put it on, using the warmth of the gift and Gzowski's voice to counteract the brittle and lonely Sunday morning. My radiator clicks its metallic heat-wave rhythm up and into my room, past the twin Golden Pothos plants whose thick leaves are the only curtain on the living-room window, a green and translucent curtain. Maudie might nod at my pattern of sound and colour and view, checking for fit and picks, for jarring juxtapositions and complimentary codes. Perhaps she would and perhaps she wouldn't, as sometimes birds-of-a-feather choose to fly alone, as that solo raven out there is doing, riding clear supporting currents over and over, back and forth, up and down, always coming around for another look.

∗   ∗   ∗

Later in the same week, at 5 a.m. I'm awake and have left the light off, choosing to lean on an elbow so I can look out my south-facing window at the half-moon brightness on the frozen Lake of the Woods. From far out on the lake, headlights dot into view and then enlarge and stream as a pickup truck moves toward town on the winter road, driving fast. The lights are blocked for a few seconds by the small treed island on which Don and Shirley have their summer place, and then the lights re-emerge, seeming to be moving much faster as the truck gets near town, with its tunnel-beam of light angling out, blending with the flat white ice and snow. After it's gone from sight, I lean a while longer, waiting to see if I'll be visited again, and then I turn on the light, deciding to accept my allotment.

✳  ✳  ✳

Jan comes back for a few days. One of the things we do is bundle-up, as it's -25°C and blowing a gale, and then set out across the bridge to Coney Island. This is something we've done before, several times, and we both have a respect for the strength of evolving ritual. We try to find a new path, new to us, around the little hill on the west end of the island, but we only come to houses as we follow snow-packed paths. We move along one path after Jan at a cross-roads, without comment or question, has followed an aging family maxim that directs, "When in doubt, turn left." A woman comes toward us, her face covered to the eyes in a scarf. Jan and I nod to her and say "Hi," but she doesn't respond in any way, no sound, no gesture, no eye-contact, nothing. This takes some doing on a narrow island snow-path, on a blowing cold January day; it requires focus. After very few steps we come to a house at the end of the path, probably the woman's house since she came from here. Strangers going toward your house on a dead-end winter path do not deserve recognition, a counter-balancing maxim, one we'll choose to forget, if we can.

We don't find a new route so go back to the central trail, with its way winding between an old brick and stone fireplace and a large rock, up a short, steep, slippery hill and along through the top-of-the-hill-woods and down the also steep other side, where you have to run down in heavy clumping boots or fall skidding on your ass. We wander awhile, exploring, finding cul-de-sacs we haven't come to before, and then we go back towards home in a hurry, now over-taken by cold.

On the walking-bridge we pause to look up and see the lights we left on in my living room, a reassuring and strange sight. We are there and we are not there; we will be there. Patterns.

*Kenora, Ontario*

# Woods and Water

*"What can have enticed me to this desolate country except the wish to stay here?"*

*— Kafka*

*"Off we go, Rocky, into the fucking woods and water . . . "*

*— Lord Harry,*
*with resignation,*
*following another golf ball*

# Dark Harbour Dulse

*T*o my surprise, I find that I'm searching for Cicely. For years I've watched runs and reruns of the American TV show *Northern Exposure*, set in the fictional Alaskan village of Cicely, finding that it not only entertained with humour and well-hidden or slapstick profundities, but that it also comforted. This inclination to watch was itself confusing to me. What does it mean to find a "situation comedy" speaking to you in a soothing way? Can institutionalization be far behind?

The connection came in the apparently accidental but deeply connected way that so many answers come, while having a Greek beer at the Plaza restaurant in Kenora. A friend had written from the Maritimes to ask what my favourite town in Canada was, and what made it special. Sitting in the booth, eating fine food and nursing beer as I answered her letter, was the first time I realized that I am in search of Cicely, a town where the inhabitants are open to magic, are finally forgiving and connected, and have generosity and humour to guide them. It would be so easy to then add, "obviously, a fantasy town," as most of us are not from nor have ever been in such a place, or that's how it seems. In Cicely, they give each other a break, so that when things get tough there is a genuine attempt to keep the show going. This seems rare.

It dawned on me, now liberated by Greek fluids, that as I drift around to North Rustico/PEI, Banff/Alberta, Mayne Island/BC, Pickle Lake/Ontario, Whitehorse/Yukon, Saskatoon/Saskatchewan, Grand Manan/New Brunswick, Victoria Beach/Manitoba, Black Tickle/Labrador and Halls Harbour/Nova Scotia, I'm looking for a town where they actually think about issues and about each other and about the real hearts of the matter, will occasionally smile you in the eye, and if your back is against the wall they'll stand clear, if you'll only let them. Tell me this is a fool's search; I dare you.

∗   ∗   ∗

When my sister Sue and I were kids in Nova Scotia, living in Pictou so that Dad had easy access to PEI on the ferry and to New Brunswick, Cape Breton and the rest of the mainland Maritimes by road, in the summer we would often go to Meteghan, our mother's home, on the "French Shore" between Digby and Yarmouth. Dad would drive us there, about an eight-hour haul on the winding slow-speed roads of then, and we would stop in the Annapolis Valley to visit his family on the way. After Mom died I spent much more time in the Valley and became more familiar with Canning, Medford, Kingsport, and Halls Harbour, and with my father's family. The time I'm talking about, and the connection with Cicely and dulse, is the time before Mom died, when most summers meant a trip to Meteghan, and it is Grand Manan dulse that makes me think of these.

When Sue and I would be getting ready to come back to Pictou from Meteghan, packing our bags at our grandparents' house where we stayed, we would always ask if we could bring home dry fish and dulse, our two favourites. Dry fish is (or was, because I don't know if it is still made; I may find out) lightly salted cod-fish, air dried and then salted just enough that it would keep in a cool cupboard for a long time but not so much that it had to be soaked before being eaten. Indeed, not – one could just tear off dry and hard chunks of fish, quickly inspect for bones, and then eat away, to be followed later by gallons of grand-parent-generated Kool-Aid, grape or raspberry depending on personal preference. We also loved to eat lobsters and clams and periwinkles and mussels, fish chowder and fried mackerel, clam broth and lobster brains, (if that is what the mushy green stuff is; we liked to think so), but we especially loved hard dulse that could be chewed for at least five minutes.

Dulse is an edible seaweed, purple, tasting of salt and aging fish, and it is gathered and sun-dried along the shores of the Bay of Fundy. It might also be gathered on the French Shore, or we may have been eating dulse from up around Digby, I have no idea. (There is always the possibility that I'll take the time and make the chance to find out all these things, later.) The more recently dulse has been gathered, and if it is then kept only in a paper bag instead of those awful little plastic grocery store bags, the more likely it is to be firm, nautically flagrant in taste, and rubbery when vigorously chewed, requiring extra volumes of saliva before it is fragmented enough to permit swallowing.

Dulse is an acquired taste, and if you haven't acquired the taste by being fed a pureed mixture as a babe, supplied in a bottle bootlegged to you between breast feeds, then you will never crave it as a part of your daily diet. In fact, you'll run screaming from the room whenever a former loved one cracks open a large paper bag of the stuff, drenching the room with the aroma of rotting fish. For those who are tempted, let me inflame this bravado by pointing out that dulse is an excellent source of iron and iodine, should you be lacking either and contemplating anemia or a goitre, has remarkably few calories, and being potently hydrophilic it is also a wonderfully explosive laxative. This latter virtue is often omitted from the grocery store's sales pitch.

Sue and I would always ask if we could bring dry fish and dulse back home to Pictou, and on receiving the ritualistic "No" we would smuggle it into our bags, stuffed between our clothes. There is something overwhelmingly evocative about the odour of unwrapped dry fish when combined with loose dulse and unwashed periwinkle and mussel shells, all captured in the pores of a "good" sweater. My sister and I were amazed that we never got caught; parents are some dumb.

*   *   *

Sue and I spent the first decade of our lives living in Pictou, a ship-building town on the Northumberland Strait, a short summer drive from the beaches of Waterside and a mere twenty-kilometre ferry ride away from Prince Edward Island. We became acclimatized to water, so when we moved with our father and adopted mother Terry to the inland town of Kentville it seemed strange, dry, cut off from essential waves. Being inland, and being cut off for that matter, is a relative thing, and we were only twenty kilometres from the coast of the Bay of Fundy, the same distance we'd previously had separating us from PEI. In the same way that we had declined to swim to PEI, we now declined to walk to the towns and beaches of Halls Harbour, Ross's Creek, Scots Bay, Medford, and Kingsport. We were inland, and we'd better get used to that, so we did. My father's family was in Canning, much nearer to the water than barren Kentville, and as we were truly related to these kin we visited often, especially to Medford and Ross's Creek and occasionally to Halls Harbour, where you could always get lobsters and dulse.

*   *   *

The Bay of Fundy is a narrow inlet of the Atlantic Ocean, separating Nova Scotia from New Brunswick but not by much, and then split-ting into the Minas Basin and Cobequid Bay on one side of Nova Scotia's Parrsboro peninsula and Chignecto Bay on the other side. As I write that, I realize that the words don't give any reasonable image of the convolutions of the coasts, the capes and harbours, bays and points. The only way to get the feel of those is to go by foot or boat, bike or even car, to feel the twists and rises yourself. A walk on the beach is worth more than a thousand pictures.

The narrowness of the Bay of Fundy produces the world's highest tides, going up and down by as much as fifteen metres, leaving the boats of Halls Harbour, for example, completely beached and leaning on their curved sides when the tide is out. Ben recently gave me an eccentric atlas, *The Reader's Digest Canadian Book of the Road*, and in section #156 it says this about Halls Harbour:

> "Overlooking the Minas Channel, where Fundy tides reach world-record heights, this picturesque fishing village is named for the captain of the pirate ship *Mary Jane*. Twice in the early 1800s he successfully raided the settlement. But on the third raid, his crew was defeated by settlers who seized the pirate gold. Legend says the loot was buried ashore, but the location is unknown . . ."

The shallow inlets and these high tides give a spectacular exodus of water, up to a kilometre and a half of beach and mudflats at Medford, for instance. You can spend a wonderful length of time just getting out to the distant edge of water, and then when the tide starts back in you can actually walk along with it, the world is tilting that fast. The tides of the Fundy give the beaches a purpose, a challenging usefulness, just to keep up, and to not get caught.

\* \* \*

*O*ne of the pleasures of growing up in the Maritimes was the opportunity to listen to the weather reports, as they changed quickly and told of actual impending bursts of excitement. They gave information about exotic places that were beside us, unknown and probably never to be seen, but right there beside us, nevertheless. Travels close to home, those in the vicinity of the mind, are the most challenging and rewarding ones, if we have the stamina to get there. I grew up hearing the weather predictions and realities for the Baccaro Banks and Anticosti, Cape Sable and Chedabucto Bay, the Bras d'Ors and the Cabot Strait, without having the slightest clue where they were or how to get there. This seemed appropriate.

Among the places I heard of as a kid were the islands of Grand Manan and Campobello and Deer Island, a trio of places, all three near to the coasts of New Brunswick and Maine at the mouth of the Bay of Fundy, but that was all I knew until I went to med school. While there during one March break, a fellow student and friend asked me to visit her home on Deer Island. It was a spectacular place, the ferry ride to get there, my friend's home and family, the proximity to the ocean, all of it.

I was told on the Deer Island trip that the best place in the world for dulse was Grand Manan, just next door. I had always thought that either Halls Harbour or Meteghan was the world capital for dulse, and so I articulated some parochial scepticism. Nope, I was told, wrong again. Grand Manan is where the purple seaweed is born, the heartland, the centre of the dulse universe. I decided immediately that I'd visit Grand Manan, when the weather report made it accessible.

\* \* \*

Medical types of people go to meetings, unending series of meetings where narrow wisdom is exchanged and gathered, and where social contracts are initiated and renewed. For several years, I have been a medical type of person, for better and for worse. At one of these party-'til-you-drop conferences, when I was living far away from the Maritimes, I was lucky enough to talk with a nurse from Grand Manan. I gushed away about missing the ocean and sea-soaked attitudes and seafood, especially clams, mussels, lobsters, and dulse. Say no more, she said, and gave me the address for Joanne and Jerry

Flagg, without even needing to look it up or call anyone. They would supply all my edible seaweed needs, or so she promised. I live in a state of cautious pessimism, so the letter I eventually mailed, on returning home to the land-locked prairie, didn't carry much hope. Within a very few weeks, back came the dulse, loose and fresh and clean, in a large paper bag, and Joanne had thrown in a jar of dulse flakes to be added to chowders, as a gift. My resolve to visit Grand Manan increased.

*　*　*

Benita and I have been taking holidays together for several years, in British Columbia, on the highways from Winnipeg and Kenora to BC and Toronto and Banff and Minneapolis, to PEI, back to BC over and over again, and on a cruise ship from Texas to Mexico and Honduras. We make many deposits in the image bank, and occasionally we get tired. This summer, we decide to do it differently, partly because we have to. Ben is working on her PhD and is behind the schedule a recalcitrant universe has set for her, while I have a manuscript to produce for a publisher who has rare spasms of remembering that I exist. The world wants us to take a working holiday, and since we are always compliant, we say "ok." We decide that we will sit in one place for at least two weeks, that we won't have a car, and that we must have enough room for both of us to write and read and think in solitude, as well as having our own shared kitchen, all the while enjoying the damn holiday.

Books come to the rescue, as they sometimes do. First, I search the map of Canada (financial and time realities have eliminated Iceland, Greece, northern Norway, and Dawson City, Yukon), looking for retreats of no-renown, and this brings me back to BC's Gulf Islands and the Atlantic provinces, all vying for the glory of our company, even though they don't know it. In section #144 of my *Book of the Road*, headlined as "A Storybook Island Off a Coast of Sheltered Coves," a paragraph on Grand Manan placed beside a map of the island, which is shaped like a sea horse and shows only about thirty-five kilometres of highway in total, says this:

> "Geological curiosities and the unhurried pace of life are among the attractions of picturesque Grand Manan, the biggest (142 square kilometres) of the Fundy isles. Local inhabitants harvest dulse (an edible seaweed) and trap lobsters.
>
> "There are no neon signs or public drinking places here. But there are tranquil forests of spruce, balsam, birch and poplar; awesome cliffs; craggy trails, bright with wildflowers; and off the sheltered east shore a forest of underwater tree stumps.
>
> "Grand Manan is a fine place for whale watching, beachcombing or basking on a lonely stretch of seaside sand."

Cicely move over, here comes Grand Manan: dulse, lobster, no neon, local inhabitants (as opposed to the other type), whales, lonely basking, awesome trails and craggy cliffs and tranquil forests and (one assumes) meandering clichés, underwater tree stumps, and (last and least) no public drinking places. I'm hooked, by history and promotional writing, and I'm able to convince Ben this would suit her too but only, I'm told, *if* there is a place of adequate size, comfort and affordability. (I highlight the "no public drinking places," and this gathers some grace.)

My research shifts into Stage Two. (I'm a trained professional, as opposed to the other type.) In Anne Hardy's snobbish yet astute guidebook *Where to Eat in Canada*, I find this commentary (after all the I'm-a-gourmet-and-you're-not blather about the coulis of wasabi and the curried mussel soup) on Grand Manan's Inn at Whale Cove:

> "The Inn is half a mile up the Whistle Road, a cluster of weathered buildings overlooking the

sea. People have been coming here to stay for a century, and Willa Cather once owned one of the cottages. Laura Buckley and her mother, Kathleen, have renovated the kitchen and the bedrooms and filled the sitting-room with antique Shaker furniture. If you stay here you'll get the feel of the old Grand Manan, when ferries were few and visitors from the mainland scarce."

While we don't want to stay for a century, and I can't remember if I have actually read Willa Cather or only studied her, Anne Hardy includes a phone number and I make the call, on a snowy March day in Kenora, the best type of day to plan a summer vacation. Laura Buckley and I exchange phone messages for a couple of weeks, and then the non-recorded voices finally connect. We agree that the Inn and cottages wouldn't fit what we're looking for, but Ms. Buckley has another place, an older house called "Uncle Dan's" in the town of North Head, and it's ours if we want it. We do.

\* \* \*

We fly into New Brunswick's St. John Airport late one evening in mid-August. On the way into town I ask the taxi driver if he knows how to get to Blacks Harbour, the terminal for the ferry to Grand Manan. He says the best way is by taxi and then adds, "Pick me!" holding up his hand in the front seat, school pupil fashion. We book a pickup for the next morning.

The next morning, I make a momentous cosmetic decision on a whim, one that has been marinating for a while, but a whim, nevertheless. This is a mistake. I haven't had my beard off in over thirty years, and since I'm now officially on holidays and don't have to worry about my naked face offending anyone, I decide to find out what is under the beard. The result is strange and not at all reassuring. There's a smaller chin than I remembered, as well as another new folding one under that tiny original, and a long thin upper lip between fatter cheeks and corner-of-the-mouth jowls. The most startling thing is how much I look like my father. I am fifty-seven and my father died when he was fifty-one, so as I look at my non-hairy face for the first time since 1968, there is an older version of my father looking back at me. It is not me. I am freaked. In fact, I'm doubly freaked, because as well as being rattled by my resemblance to my father, I'm also dismayed by the extent of my vanity.

Quickly, as fast as hair will grow, I decide to return to my hairy persona, the one that allows me to shape my face as I see fit all the while pretending that it's a political statement. I'm hoping enough will grow back in the two weeks I'm hiding out on an island off the coast of New Brunswick so that no one will suspect that the bare-faced one is the real me. "What have I done?" I ask myself, glancing at a small mirror. My father looks back at me, saying nothing.

In the lobby of the St. John hotel, at the designated *pick-me-*pickup time, the taxi driver looks right through me. I introduce my-self, and he recoils in shock, saying "What the *hell?* You've changed, and not for the better," or that's how I translate the look on his face. We set out for Blacks Harbour, which as well as being a ferry termi-nal is also the place where tinned fish grow, where sardines and her-ring are laid to rest in easy-to-open cans. We talk with the cabbie and he is good at his jobs, both of them, the driving part and the keeping the fares happy part. It also seems that he is a good guy, that's my guess. We get to Blacks Harbour, drive through the famous cannery town and pull up at the base of a long wide wharf, in full sunshine, waiting for the ferry.

It is a hot day, and Ben and I have a lot of stuff with us, in prep-aration for all the writing, studying, walking, and at-home drinking and basking we're going to do over the next two weeks. The cab driver speaks to someone who works for the ferry company, someone he knows, and we are then told to pile our luggage on a trolley that they produce for us and advised where to look for it on the ship, on the car level. Foot passengers are expected to carry everything on and off the ferry, and I had been planning to make two or three trips to get it on board, so this is a welcome reprieve. I'm appropriately appreciative with the cabbie, and ask him to pick us up, right here in Tin Fish City, two weeks to the day. He agrees.

The *Grand Manan V* comes in slowly. It is mostly white, with a red hull and red stripes, and with yellow and black smokestacks and towers. It isn't nearly as large and grand as the ones in BC, so things are already shaping up to be excellent. We load ourselves onto the ferry. On the way I meet the man who has taken on our luggage by the trolley, and I ask him if it would be acceptable for me to give him some money, as a thank-you for doing this. He looks me in the eye and says no, but he doesn't seem to be offended, so I've asked the right way.

We take pictures of each other on the ship, leaning on the railing in our t-shirts and bare faces and shades, basking, genuine tourists. On the ninety-minute trip across, we see porpoises leaping, and several fishing boats, and Grand Manan being brought closer by our movement. It is wonderful to be adrift on the Bay of Fundy again.

\* \* \*

Laura Buckley eventually meets us at the wharf in North Head, after a short wait on our part in which we find there are no taxis and that "Uncle Dan's place" is within walking distance. It will only take us a few killer trips to lug everything to "the red house just up the road, not long after the Compass Rose." Ms. Buckley arrives and is a woman of few words, six maybe seven, and I'm pleased to be self-consigned to the backseat as we get quickly shown the town and her place at Whale Cove, before being checked into Uncle Dan's place. It's a wonderful old house, with two bedrooms and a bathroom upstairs, all with windows looking out over Long Island Bay on the upper east side of the island. It has a large kitchen and huge living room downstairs, as well as a windowed veranda. There is a wraparound deck on the side of the house facing the bay, and from here we can see the town's wharf and anchored boats, and fishing boats going both ways in and out of the harbour. We've done the right thing.

Laura Buckley leaves, having to get cooking for the Inn's evening meal she says, and advising us to pay before we leave in two weeks. There is no paperwork. We walk through the house a couple of times, getting a feel for it, and then start to settle and to negotiate about space. I'll get to work at a small drop-leaf desk in the far end of the living room, and Ben will get the larger but less cute kitchen table. We're both happy. The clothes get unpacked and put in drawers, suitcases stowed, books distributed, lists of needs made, the view admired from every possible angle, and then we go exploring.

North Head has only a few hundred people, my size of town, and it also has a grocery store and a bakery, where we stock up, and several hotels, gift-shops and restaurants, including the Compass Rose that Laura Buckley has already pointed out. (From my observational back-seat position in Ms. Buckley's car, as she whirled us around, I had asked about good places to eat "near where we'll be," as her place at Whale Cove was a healthy walk away. I wanted to hear what she'd say about her competition. She hesitated, but not for long, and then pointed at the Compass Rose, saying it was only a five-minute walk from Uncle Dan's. Good on you, I thought.) There's also a Post Office and a large, high, working wharf, jammed with fishing boats on this Sunday afternoon. There's not a liquor store in sight, and when I ask at the bakery I'm told we'll have to go to Castalia, "on the way to Grand Harbour." I also ask about Joanne and Jerry Flagg's dulse place, and receive some complicated turn-here-and-there directions, leading me to nod knowingly and thank the person, and then ignore the whole exchange; I'll find them later.

That evening we dress up somewhat, nothing overwhelming, and walk slowly in the heat up a hill to The Inn at Whale Cove for dinner, as we'd arranged with Laura Buckley. We follow the shorter back-door route she had suggested, going by the actual watery cove, and then along a path through a short stretch of woods before coming out to the cottages and main building. It's excellent, elevated, looking out over the water and a point of land opposite. There's a table reserved for us. We like the waiter and the wine is good, and I once again make a mental genuflection towards the much-maligned Anne Hardy, she of nose-in-the-air-while-telling-us-where-to-eat fame. She has some wonderful-good taste buds, does Anne. Since I'm on an I-beg-your-pardon roll, I aim one at Laura Buckley, who may not bother with charming chatter because she's on a higher plane, wondering what the gods would like to eat, and wondering if we are worthy of her skills. We eat and drink well and then weave our way home in the dark, congratulating ourselves for knowing how to live.

∗   ∗   ∗

We have a work plan. This involves getting up at 6:30 a.m., "7 a.m. at the latest," getting showered, having breakfast, in my case having a whole pot of coffee, and then getting down to separate and serious work by 8 a.m. For most of the two weeks we do this, and we are very impressed with ourselves. We usually go straight through until lunch at noon, then work again from 1 to 3 p.m. After that we're on our own, workplace obligations be damned. Then we go for walks and shopping, mail letters and postcards, but mostly we explore.

Grand Manan is a sloping island, higher with steep cliffs on the west side, the back of the sea horse shape that is turned toward New Brunswick, and with low shores and many sheltered coves and bays on the east side, the front of the sea horse that faces Nova Scotia but from farther away. For much of the last two centuries there were many shipwrecks along the coast of this rocky island, especially on the west side, and as a result there are now hiking trails at the water's edge, high up on the cliffs in many cases, remnants of the old rescue and salvage trails.

We get a brochure showing these hiking trails, and one of them goes from Whale Cove, on the east side of the cove opposite the Inn, along the coastal edge of a thick and long point of land to come out at Swallowtail Lighthouse on the outskirts of North Head, a few kilometres past the ferry terminal. There is also a hiking trail shown for Dark Harbour, on the steep west side of the island, at the end of the only road going across. As I've been told that Dark Harbour dulse is the best in the world, this is a walk I have to take. We also get to create walks of our own, over and over to the high and busy wharf, along the highway to the bakery, through the town and then up to the Swallowtail Lighthouse, and along the rocky beach in either direction in front of our house, which is not ours at all but Ms. Buckley's and before her Uncle Dan's place, now red and with the number 105 on the side facing the road. We take most of these walks in the afternoon, and plan to take more.

\*　\*　\*

On one of our late afternoon hikes we have gone across the street from our place, up a steep driveway through the grounds of a church, and down an eventually unpaved lane that extends from the church past some houses and on to the east side of Whale Cove. This cove is wide and sweeping in a grandly curved way, with an entirely rocky shore, not a grain of sand in sight, instead having unending small weatherworn smoothed rocks. We wander along the top of the driftwood and by the water's edge, looking for paths of any kind, avoiding bothering the large number of seagulls. On one of the first evenings of our stay, we see a car sitting over by the far end of the cove, nearer to the path that leads up through the woods to the Inn. We end up near this car, and we speak to the family, a man and a woman and an older child. There is a sign taped to the back window of the car advertising car rentals. We've been told that there are no car rentals available on Grand Manan, so we pounce, and right there arrange for a phone call tomorrow with Betty. It turns out that we'll be able to rent a car any time we want to, and we do want to, two or three times for sure.

A couple of days later we get a none-too-clean and none-too-solid neo-relic rental car, which fits us. We drive the top-to-tail roads of the island, going up the hill to the Swallowtail Lighthouse and then on to the end of the road on the north end at Ashburton Head.

There's another lighthouse here, and a foghorn, close and loud. We then come back through the town of North Head, noting a couple of houses for sale and slowing to evaluate, to consider the thought, before going along the road which runs the length of the east side of the island, close to the water, to Southwest Head. We go through Castalia and Woodwards Cove, Grand Harbour and Seal Cove, taking detours into the towns and along the road to Ingalls Head where the ferry goes to the small island of White Head. Then we move on to the now-discovered larger grocery store and the liquor store. At Southwest Head we park the car and wander along the sightseeing paths, to the lighthouse and cliff edge. We've talked with the owner of a more remote and smaller cottage, which only can be reached by walking a path toward Hay Point, and we consider walking that way, but then decide against it. We also decide to save for later the drive to Dark Harbour, on the only road to the west side of the island.

In Grand Harbour we've stopped by a small hotel, so close to the water that the deck of the place is a functioning wharf, and have asked if we could see rooms and dining room, for some other time when we will come here again. They give us keys and let us look about. Later, as we're leaving, two people walk by our car in the parking lot, as we are pulling away. I went to school with the man thirty years ago, but in my new fresh-faced persona I am unrecognizable. We keep driving.

∗   ∗   ∗

Early in our first week the fog settles in, and I mean this in a literal way. It is dense, unmoving, enveloping to an extreme degree, and very comforting. I grew up with fog, especially in Pictou and Halls Harbour, and even sometimes in the deep interior of the arid Annapolis Valley where I lived. Fog is an attitudinal challenge, along with everything else, and I am blessed to perceive it as a comfort blanket, a chance to sit back with the metaphoric or actual fireplace and let the world calm down because it has to. There is no choice but to drive slowly and forget about the conflict over walks versus work or whether it is possible to find an even higher vantage point for a great view; all of that goes away as the fog settles in. There is no choice. We feel safe in Uncle Dan's house in the fog; there is no risk to our stay here. It is difficult to imagine that we will ever see the sun again.

We do go for walks on the several days in a row where fog has wrapped us, and my favourite is to watch the *Grand Manan V* come and go. Watching it leave is a gift of spectral reality, as it backs out into the fog before straightening and then easing out of sight, with seagulls cruising around it. The fog blinds to depth and distance and it muffles sound; it is better at its work than is night darkness.

\* \* \*

The fog lifts and the sun lifts up our eyes. In spite of myself I'm elated by this return of distance, so we decide to take the whole afternoon and go for a hike. The trail from Whale Cove to the Swallowtail Lighthouse takes us about three hours, as we stop to admire the Hole-in-the-Wall, several weirs, a few viewpoints with benches and many others without. We take our time, stopping for lunch from our backpacks, admiring the aloofness of the cliffs and forest and enjoying the loud-voiced seagulls, and then as we near the end of the trail watching the *Grand Manan V* and several fishing boats sail north before turning west toward the Grand Manan Channel. The sun keeps on shining, and it is difficult to imagine that fog will ever again exist.

It is startling to see functioning weirs again, my first in many years, and unexpected to me so far away from the mainland coast. This makes me realize that I don't understand how either weirs or tides function, and I spend some time trying to catch up. When I was a kid in the Annapolis Valley of Nova Scotia, these enclosures of stakes and netting with one narrow opening were seen on the Bay of Fundy. The receding tides trap the fish and allow the fishers to walk or drive out and pick them out of the nets, easy pickings with your feet planted on the mudflats. There are many of these weirs in the coves and on the edges of Grand Manan, and it is a welcome sight from my past to watch them used again and to try to figure out how and why they empty them here from boats rather than on foot. It comes to me; I eventually get it. This is *not* a tourist's museum piece. It is functioning, a genuine fishing island. It's good to see us tourists lose one, for a change.

\*   \*   \*

In the summer on Saturday mornings, from ten to noon, there is a Farmers' Market at North Head. We are there at 10:05 a.m., not wanting to appear overly eager, and separately we amble from stall to stall. Most of the market is outdoors in the parking lot between the Business Centre and the Provincial Court building, with a few overflow tables also set up inside the courthouse. There are about fifteen tables and stalls in total, with about fifty shoppers and browsers circulating. It is sunny, with just the right degree of cool ("much like ourselves," I opine in a low voice to Ben.) People appear to be relaxed, casually talking and at the same time looking at used books, knitted sweaters, vegetables, photographs, leather belts, soaps, jams, and cakes and cookies. Everything is homemade, homegrown or home-found, everything.

I buy a leather belt from a man who has two racks of belts he has made, one of "seconds" for $5 and one of thicker belts with better buckles and no visible imperfections for $50. I decide that I can live with the imperfections and hand over $5, holding up the one beige belt I want. The bearded man, who is about my age, glances at my body, then grins at me and says I might want one of the longer ones so it will go around my middle. I mock-scowl at him, reluctantly admit he's right, and exchange it for a longer one.

We talk. He's originally from Canning, Nova Scotia, where my father grew up, and he knows my uncles and aunts and cousins. He and his partner left Canning years ago, travelling across Canada and working as they went to finance the next move, getting as far west as Vancouver before they got seriously down-homesick. At this point, the two of them made a deal. The agreement was that the first one to land a job in the Maritimes would leap at it, and the other would accompany, right away, not later. (This awkward necessity of earning a living is the difficult part of returning to the east coast, or to most of rural Canada in general, and I hear variations on this story over and over again, all across the country.) His wife got a job teaching on Grand Manan so here they came and here they will stay, only about 200 kilometres from Canning by seagull route. He invites me back to buy one of the better belts, "when you win the lottery." I agree.

Finally, I stop at a table where jars of strawberry-rhubarb jam and bags of homemade cookies are being sold by a mother and son. They look alike, with direct eyes and smiles, and the same round faces and bodies. Looking at them, I miss my daughters and wish they could visit this Farmers' Market on this morning, so we could walk and watch and talk. The boy is about thirteen or fourteen, and he seems happy to be here, on a Saturday morning in August, selling jam and cookies, making change and talking with strangers. This strikes me as unusual, and then I'm ashamed of myself. I buy a jar of jam for $2, more in recognition of their admirable style than from need.

Later that day, Ben and I are in Grand Harbour, touring in our second-day rental car from Betty. We stop to get cash at the Scotia Bank's ATM, having gone berserk with our $7 purchases (each) at the market. As we are entering the bank, the same mother and son are leaving, and I say, "Did you sell all of your things?" They come close to recognizing me, smiling and saying, "Almost all." They both look happy.

The accompanying story I concoct, as we drive home from the bank and the Spend-More grocery store, is this: the mother is clever, and she has made an arrangement with her son. He learns how to make jam and cookies, and then they will sell these at the market all summer, with the money going into his bank account every Saturday afternoon. (All the money or only a share? Who knows? I can only get so far in my fantasies.) What doesn't get sold will get eaten at home. There is also the matter of sharing the time, watching and talking together. I tell Ben my version of the scene, as she drives us home, and she smiles and says, "Good story." I can't tell if she believes it.

I make plans, this time with more conviction and detail, to buy a better belt and more jam, the next time I'm here.

✳   ✳   ✳

Time speeds up when you don't want it to, and that's the only time it does. We are both working effectively and consistently, every day from 8 a.m. to about 3 p.m., and we're also occasionally feeling bored and one-dimensional and wasted. Ghosts and social approval be damned, what's a Grand Manan for, if not to have a grand time? We need to get out more, on this second week of proximity to salt water, so we do.

The beach in front of Uncle Dan's house is wide and rocky, with the town of North Head and its wharf at one end, and miles of walking at the other. We begin to pick the miles of walking. Most days the shore is almost empty of people, with a couple of hot-day exceptions when the sand beach a few hundred metres from our place is packed with about ten kids and a smaller number of parents. On the cooler days, the very few people we encounter are interesting.

There's a large man, with white hair, an open face and a matching large open voice, who is a geologist. He is enthused that we are interested in the origins and evolutionary details of the stones and cliffs we have wandered over, especially when I blurt out that Ben has a PhD in the making. This revelation doesn't win me any points with Benita. In fact, I can probably count on some MD-revealing retaliation, but it excites the hell out of Buddy, and when I ask the questions he answers directly to Ben. (Another victory for the PhDs over the MDs. Our MD fee-for-service rates are still so much more advantageous, though, even if the advantage is not for society.) He gives us considerable detail, and while we forget it within days it does add to the pleasure of the walks, although it doesn't change which rocks we gather to keep or place on the deck railing at the house. We picks them because we likes them, as Labradoreans might say, and that's that.

The same day we get our rock lesson, we go further along the shore and startle a woman who is taking pictures of the rocks. This initially almost pisses her off, but B and I are on a social-skills roll, and we apologize and smile and charm our way out of it, so that she puts down the camera and talks with us. I like this talk much better, because she'd rather not be doing it, so the ideas and details don't come gushing out of her, but they do come. She has decided that we're worth some time and so communicates honestly, with eye contact and smiles and words that mean something.

She is trying to take pictures of this particular section of large-rocked beach in order to create an illusion. The rocks here have water-caused downhill swirls, (and this connects to the geology we've just been taught, but we let that recede), and they have patches of hanging seaweed that could look like spruce trees if seen from back-a-ways. She is trying to find an angle that would make the viewer of her picture be unable to distinguish this view from a mountain landscape, one taken without the giveaway of context or perspective. We see what she means, but it is difficult, involving finding just the right distance and angle, as does our talk with her.

She was brought up on the island, and doesn't seem to mind being asked about that, so we cautiously probe how it made her, and how it affects her now when she cares to visit and take photos. Her partner would rather stay away and does just that. I tell her where I'm from, just across the way, and we talk briefly about conservatism and change and the limits of both. For the first time, talking with this woman creating a mountain on the beach, I think there is a possibility I could live on Grand Manan, for some time. We leave her to herself, and she seems to appreciate that, but not too much, not enough to hurt our feelings.

Farther along, after close to an hour's scrambling over slippery rocky points and then coming to a very long tiered section of small-stoned beach, we see two people sitting, way up ahead. As we get closer it appears that they have been sunning and we've intruded, leading them to put on some clothes. Having been known to wander naked on beaches ourselves, we feel badly about this, but there is no way to convey naked ease at four hundred metres, so we just accept the cover-your-taboo-parts rule of the society, and walk toward them.

They are from Poland, a man and a woman, one older, my age, and one younger, and it doesn't matter which is which, not to me it doesn't. (I'm making up for my shame from the Saturday morning jam and cookies judgments.) My daughter Jan has just come back from dancing in Europe, spending time in Finland, Austria, Sweden, and Germany, but mostly in Poland, living in Gdansk for several months. The city and the country were not friendly to Jan and her dancing colleagues, most of them weren't, most of the time, and as we stand and talk I wish they had met these two, because they are wonderful and Jan would have liked them. We talk about how they came to be on Grand Manan, from Poland, and which restaurants and drives have been enjoyed, and what we all do with our lives. They are confident, friendly, open, and thoughtful. We talk, all four of us, and enjoy it.

They are bothered by the lack of public access to the beaches and shoreline here, and we quickly and sincerely agree with them, realizing as we do that we have simply ignored or circumvented the access barriers, often without thinking about it. This would not be so easy or comfortable if we were visiting a small island off the coast of Poland. We apologize on behalf of the Canadian, New Brunswick, and Grand Manan governments; they laugh, and accept our apologies. An international incident has been avoided.

We go back to walking, reluctant to leave them and hoping to meet up again at a restaurant. We are also hoping their clothes are removed again, before the sun and interpersonal warmth goes away.

\* \* \*

As a part of our retreat from dedication to work we increase our exploration of the dining rooms in North Head by going to the Compass Rose and two other hotels on successive evenings, using Buckley's Inn at Whale Cove as the gold standard. She is the best, the giant in a land of seafood superstars, as we decide that you just can't find a bad seafood dinner here. On one occasion, at the Compass Rose, two American couples *do* complain about the small size of their portions, but we figure that this must be a desperation move, a hail-Mary, last-second, last-down attempt, as there is so little else to carp about, and we elite tourists must maintain our fighting edge. The waiter and owner and kitchen staff obviously see the complaint in the same light, accepting that an American's got to do what an American's got to do. They ignore the comment, pay it no mind whatsoever. This close to the USA, we seem to be getting loads of free trade in cultural stereotypes, and I applaud this as progress.

At Laura Buckley's place we talk with our server, who is here from Europe with her partner, who is himself working with the fishery for some months. They are going to be moving along soon, and she says while she will miss the island, she is tired. This is a busy dining room, one of the best east of Toronto, and she is hustling. Jan earns her daily bread, and daily car and apartment, by doing this work in Calgary, Toronto and Winnipeg, and it is hard work. She has said that receiving healthy tips takes some of the sting out of a server's life, which leans towards being chronically stung, so we tip well. Our server agrees with Jan, and appreciates us.

Laura Buckley does all the cooking, which perhaps explains her taciturn approach. She is a wizard, producing delicious lobster ravioli and crab cakes, spectacular salmon and scallops, and bread that itself is worth the price of admission. We are becoming increasingly captivated by Grand Manan, and this is the dangerous stage in the ongoing search for Cicely.

When we visited British Columbia's Mayne Island and the North Rustico area of PEI, we also became captivated and called the real estate people. So long as we keep these discussions restricted to the dream-on variety, we're safe. This annoys the real estate people but must, after all, be one of the necessary hazards of the trade. It's when you start to get serious that you're in serious trouble. In spite of this, Ben makes the call and we get the information, the lots and housing availability and prices, waterfront and not, in town and way the hell out and gone, the works. The emotional stakes jump, as this is an affordable place. As opposed to Mayne Island, where the prices were astronomical and therefore led to instant relief because there was no way to even consider buying, Grand Manan *is* affordable. The ferry probably keeps away the chronic dreamers and weekend gamblers, as it should, and it also keeps the prices down.

Dreams can get you into debt, and so can conceptual Cicely. We decide to come back again, and to think about it between now and then. There's no seer like a cautious dreamer.

\*   \*   \*

Getting near the middle of our second and last week, Ben springs one on me, and even though I'm surprised, my resistance forces rally and I fight back. Ben suggests that we take a boat tour, of which there are several in Grand Manan, and she specifically recommends a sailboat tour that watches whales. I dig in: our routine of early-day work followed by walking is going well, so why change it? Add to this slavery to routine, even new and short-lived routine, a dislike of sailboats with their nausea-inducing up and down and sideways tossing about, and my stranger-phobia, usually masked by bright-eyed gregarious charm but nevertheless all too real, being challenged by fifteen to twenty certified *strange* people jammed together on the damn tossing sailboat for most of a day. I put up a fine fight, I really do, full of pseudo-logic (my specialty) even though totally devoid of any flicker of sense, but there is no way to withstand the research and water-torture capabilities facing me. I'm easily defeated and we get booked on the tour.

I pray for fog and/or high wind, either of which will cancel the whole trip, but it is pointed out to me that big-haired Jewish academic non-slaves-to-routine people have a direct line to the weather gods. As a result of this unfair affiliation, the sail day comes up sunny and gentle. We motor out into the Bay of Fundy, aiming roughly towards Halls Harbour on the Nova Scotian shore, but in reality just getting out to the middle of the bay.

There are three crew members: Sarah, who is the Captain and in her late twenties or early thirties; Allan, her father and the on-deck crew member; and Sue, the cook and down-below crew member. It is a flat calm day, so we're having to use the motor and not the sails, but this will allow us to see whales and other sea animals more easily. I start to get into this, carefully hiding that fact from the inclined-to-gloat Ben, and position myself near the front of the ship, watching, pleased that we're more-or-less (mostly less, but what-the-hell) aiming toward Cape Split and Halls Harbour and Ross's Creek, toward where I belong – part of me anyway.

At first we just motor on, not seeing much, but meeting some people who are pleasant, and finding that the day is warm enough to be in shorts and sleeves-up shirt, and the sun feels wonderful on my wispy new-bearded face. No one has yet burst into uncontrollable laughter at my bare face, so I'm easing back a degree or two from my tendency to hide under the furled sails. Sue serves us strong real coffee, followed within an hour by an incredibly fine chowder. It is full of fish and shellfish, with a broth that leads me to offer money and/or hand in marriage to Sue, who declines both, but she does offer second helpings to those who have humbled themselves appropriately, as I definitely have. Life is wonderful out here on the flat-surfaced ocean, and I ask Ben why in hell we don't do this sort of thing more often, stating that she spends entirely too much time working away, a slave to academe. Ben nods, deadpan, agreeing completely.

On cue, the animals appear in sequence, I swear. We first see a small group of white-sided dolphins, jumping and following us for awhile. I ask their name, and am told. Watching them, loving their motion, I remember Don and Ruth and I being given roast "jumper" on the Labrador coast, during one of our mobile summer clinics. It was delicious. I keep this story to myself.

Allan then points and says to Sarah that he thinks he sees a basking shark, up ahead. I've never seen a basking shark, not once, and ask about them. I'm told that these are very large sharks, not dangerous carnivores, and they have a unique tendency to hang around near the surface, to bask. Sarah maneuvers us beside this creature, and it is indeed large, and it is also just lurking about on the surface. When we get right up beside it, it gets spooked or annoyed and goes under, gradually angling down and away as we watch it through the clear calm water, five metres of thick wide shark. Later on, farther up the bay, we see another one and the whole process is repeated, with us getting an even better look this time. Carnivore or not, I'd rather not bump into one of these on my next swim across the Bay of Fundy.

We have a lengthy conversation with Cathy and Philip, who have a touring company just outside Halifax, specializing in bicycle tours in many parts of the world. They used to have one for Grand Manan but have stopped it, and they're back partly as tourists and partly to reassess. They communicate well with us and with each other, are smart, strong and confident in the manner of successful entrepreneurs, and they are admiring this sailboat trip for the skillful process as well as the content, the charm and chowder and warmth as well as the dolphins and basking sharks. These two know the business, and they freely acknowledge the abilities of our captain and crew. Ben shoots another deadpan glance my way and doesn't say a word.

Allan spots whales up ahead. These are right whales, from the baleen family of whales and so-named by whalers because they were, and are, so easy to kill. As with so many species on this planet, evolution and adaptation have not included learning how to cope with the murderous skills of humans. This is a family of whales, and we see calves and one-year-olds and older adults. A couple of the animals are just hanging around on the surface, more basking, and they let the ship come within seven metres before swimming away, while others are farther out, diving with the classic arching tail-salute as they go. We spend a couple of hours watching and following them, being careful to ease into proximity, to not harass or annoy, to restrain the casual destructive tendencies of the species we are representing. The whales seem to appreciate this, tolerating us, and in a couple of one-year-old instances, coming close to get a look at us, to sightsee the gawking tourists.

I've seen many whales in the ocean, in their watery turf: humpbacks, minke, pilot, beluga, gray, and now right. Their calm majesty always moves me; it captures and converts. "Resistance is futile; prepare to be assimilated," they could say, and I'd be there, no resistance from me, none. Unfortunately for us, and more wisdom to them, they have no interest in assimilating us, and they gradually move off, leaving us to go away.

We sail for Grand Manan, capturing some breeze in our unrolled sails as the sky clouds over and the wind comes up. We have moved, and have been moved, and it is good to be going home.

*   *   *

After several partial attempts at finding Joanne and Jerry Flagg's dulse place, by asking and following convoluted instructions only to get nowhere near, we set out on a sunny afternoon near the end of our stay, and we're serious this time. We do find their house, an elevated bungalow set back from a winding side road and looking to have other buildings out back, but we can't get near any of it because of a large barking dog. We retreat. We then go in search of the ever-present plan B, starting by going across the road where we see two young boys in the yard.

"Is that dog dangerous?" I ask, willing to trust local knowledge to the bitter and rabid end. "No! Won't hurt you!"says one, with the other one adding, postscript fashion, "She bit him once, though, last year, right in the penis. I bet it hurt, too."

As I cluck sympathetically about Buddy's woofed willy, and Ben tries to hide her laughter from all males in the vicinity, we set out looking for another route to the back of the house, now accompanied by two guides. When one of them gives a good long-distance spitting exhibition, I say that Ben is the champion long-distance spitter of the entire prairie region, but she declines to respond to their challenge of proof, possibly because she has always found it difficult to stifle laughter and spit at the same time. The boys lead us round-about to the back yard of Joanne and Jerry, although it's more like a back field or a large clearing in the woods. They are there, and we introduce ourselves. Joanne remembers the name, from the mail orders and shipping.

I stand and stare, in a dulse lover's paradise. There is a large area, probably a half acre or two garden plots, *big* is the point, covered in sun-drying dulse. Joanne sees my fascination and then shows me the barn, where Jerry and another man are moving dulse around. There are high and deep piles of it, like hay in a mow, ready for bagging and sorting on the basis of quality and ready, in my case, for being stared at and inhaled. Imagine many rotting fish in an enclosed space and you've got it, the best perfume ever. Ben goes back out to watch the field of dulse dry in the sun and to breathe deeply, while I stand in the barn and watch and breathe deeply, each to his *and* her own.

It seems that Joanne is a bit surprised to have us come and see their operation, but not that surprised. She explains step-by-step how it all works, and then offers to walk with us down their path and driveway, past the perverted biting dog. Joanne reassures me that the dog isn't dangerous, but I still manage to keep my front to the wall and back to the dog as we go into the basement of her house, where the dulse orders are prepared for shipment. ("Not dangerous, harrumph," I say to Ben, when we're out of hearing range for a minute. "Easy for you vulvar types to say.") Joanne shows us some old pictures of Dark Harbour, where the seaweed is gathered, and tells us the story of the place. She asks if we've been there. Not yet, we say, but we're going, we're definitely going.

\* \* \*

The story we have heard about Dark Harbour is this: during the early decades of the twentieth century there was a community at Dark Harbour, a full-time fishing village. One winter, there was a huge storm which wiped out the village and permanently changed the landscape, making it impossible for the community to come together again, to be rebuilt. It stopped being. We are told that a few people live there now, mostly dulse gatherers and salmon farmers and recluses, and that the rocky breakwater, which partially closes off the harbour from the ocean, becomes an island when the tide comes in. If we want to walk out on the breakwater, we'll have to time our visit.

We rent a car from Betty and set out for the other side of the island. The road becomes high and twisting as we near the west coast, with a steep descent into Dark Harbour. There is a small wharf at the bottom of the hill and the end of the road, and some room by the side of the road to park the car, with a few small houses off to the right. The only access to the breakwater, where (as we all know) the world's best dulse is gathered, is by skirting the harbour along the shoreline.

We start walking around the bottom of the harbour, stepping across flat rocks to cross a shallow creek, and then go along the narrow ledge of shore toward the long finger of a rocky breakwater that is up ahead of us, several hundred metres away. Ben points out, accurately, that the tide seems to be coming in and if we aren't careful we'll get caught for the night out on the point, soon to be a rock is-land. I really want to see this place up close, and to get to the other end of the breakwater if I can, so I convince her to keep going, but not for long. When we get to the base of the breakwater, which is about a kilometre long and five to ten metres wide, terraced in rocky levels with scatters of driftwood and a few small shacks as well as one fine small house, my ability to convince Ben to outrun the tide collapses, and she turns back. I'm told that she'll come over the hill to pick me up tomorrow, when the tide goes out, if she remembers and if something else hasn't come up. Fine, just fine by me, as I'd prefer the company out here on this forlorn piece of ocean-whipped outcrop anyway, especially if that company is nobody but me. Ben starts back, and I start fast-walking for the other end of the break-water, hoping there is a way across to the other side of the harbour there, a narrow leap or a footbridge or a Tarzan vine or a stealable boat or a shallow ford, anything will do. I don't want to stay out here overnight, but mostly I don't want to become vulnerable to the rav-ages of I-told-you-so.

There are four small liveable buildings on the breakwater, and one of them is obviously lived in all the time. It has a porch and deck and windows, and has the feel of a lived-in and cared for home. I've been told before that you can't buy property out here, but that no one evicts you if you simply settle in, squat, make yourself belonged. As I walk the breakwater I am experiencing a strong at-home feel-ing, right here on the breakwater at Dark Harbour, Grand Manan. It doesn't matter to me, not at all, that I don't see a single flake or frond of dulse. If I come here often, it will make itself appear.

I go to the other end of the narrow rock finger, seeing along the way where I will put my place if I dare to adapt my life to do so. As I get to the end, I recognize that there is no way across the fast and deep current of water going through the gap of ten to twelve metres. The gap is built and maintained to allow fishing boats in and out, and people can't get across. I'm snookered.

I start back, at a hobbling trot, convinced I'm not going to be able to outrun the tide of the Bay of Fundy and yet elated, knowing that I'll be safe and OK here overnight – I'll be able to make it so. I'll be able to make it forgiving, to adapt my shape to the rocks.

I'm out of shape but not desperately, and I make pretty good time getting back to the base of the breakwater, and then really turn it on to get around the narrow shelf of a passable shoreline which the tide has now reduced to only a few centimetres, before coming to the filling creek. I manage to find some flat-rock jumps across, so that I'm not even damp, and I am chortling in my triumph over the gods of tide and doubt as I find Ben at the wharf, waiting for my body to be washed up. My I-told-you-so routine is much more subtle than that which I usually have to endure, except for my little impromptu twirling dance and rap chant, which edges towards excessive. Ben is moderately glad to see me, nevertheless, but I'm afraid that a recognition of the charms of the Dark Harbour breakwater as a potential homestead is mine alone.

As we drive back to North Head, and over the next two days as we pack and pay and then leave, it becomes clear that Grand Manan has allowed me to recognize Cicely. I realized on the breakwater, for the first time, that Cicely is in me, if I care and dare to look. I may even have the luck and the skill to have several. I'm in debt to Grand Manan and will see if I can bring Cicely along with me, next time.

*North Head, Grand Manan, New Brunswick*

# *At Sea*

*T*he first step of our departure from Canada to the USA, neigh-
bour-extraordinaire, is at the airport in Winnipeg as we go
through Customs. The American Customs people glance at
the slips and tickets and passports, but mostly they look at our faces,
at our eyes I'd bet. It's where I'd look. Overall, we go past a ticket-
agent for the airline, a customs and immigration person for the pass-
port and then another one, flanked by two guys with guns, for the
declaration slip (I declare *nothing*, and am proud of myself), and
then finally the standard-issue x-ray and metal-detecting bored and
alienated security people, which is the last glancing scrutiny before
the boarding frenzy. We are innocuous and nearing invisibility, or
cute as buttons, and we breeze through.

It is +2°C in Winnipeg, sunny and autumn, and the two of us
are still at work in our heads and reflexes and attitudes. I call
daughter-J from the airport's waiting room, missing her already. It is
a frightening thing to fly away from people you love.

✳  ✳  ✳

In Labrador, twenty-five years ago anyway, people would ask, "What'd you do on the weekend?" and the answer might be, "Went to The Islands, for a cruise." Or someone from inland North West River, on meeting a known person from coastal Rigolet on a wind-whipped Saturday in February at the Hudson's Bay Store, might say, "You just up for a cruise, or what?"

It's taken me twenty-five years, but I could now answer "yes," as I'm going on a cruise, flying from Winnipeg to Houston and then getting aboard the *M/S Norwegian Sea* for a week. Sarah is a dancer on this ship, and I'm going to be able to see her for the first time in over seven months. It is a wonderful thing to fly toward people you love.

I have plans for this trip and this visit, and they are grandiose. My plans include giving Sarah smiles and hugs but absolutely no advice or direction of any kind. She'll think I'm down with fulminating illness. In a week of sailing and docking, I'll get to see Sarah dance as part of a fourteen-member group, twice a night on three different nights. With luck and some skill, we'll also get to talk and walk and maybe lean on the ship's railing, ten stories above the sea. We'll watch for whales and dolphins, other ships passing, and mostly just for the stretch of deep salt water extending beyond the horizon, a sight I miss. That's my image of the week to come:  seven days of sunny heat, seeing much of a much-loved dancer, and leaning on the ship's port railing, watching one distant wave unfold.

\* \* \*

The Houston Airport is huge, with four terminals, a driverless subway shuttle-bus, and an elegant hotel attached, and everything goes smoothly in spite of me waiting for it to refuse.

At the airport, Ben and I have no idea where to meet the bus which will take us to the *M/S Norwegian Sea*, not a clue, so we wander about in the football-stadium-size Terminal C looking for a sign, any sign will do. There's a woman in a white and blue uniform standing casually by a middle-of-the-space conglomeration of notice boards and mini-counter obstacles. She is waiting. I assume she's an airline crewmember, so approach her to ask if she knows where the shuttle buses come in. She smiles and directs me across the terminal, but then as I thank her and turn to go she asks which one I'm looking for. "Norwegian," I say, "NCL," and she calmly redirects her pointing finger back at herself. "That's me," she says. She has been waiting for us, and about a thousand others like us. The day goes like that, with the Texas universe giving itself up, as you only wish it always would.

\*   \*   \*

The drive to the ship is humbling and metaphoric (isn't it all?), as we go through some of the most heavy-duty industrially bleak landscape I've seen in a long while. I've been warned about this by my daughters, so it just rolls off my retina, no sweat, almost none. We drive by grim and boarded-up strip-malls and others that aren't boarded up but should be, oil refineries and tank farms, and mile after mile of pre-crumbling housing. Our bias about the USA, land of the free but only if you've got the cash, is given credence by this one-hour drive through distressed land.

Many times and in different places I try to imagine what an aboriginal person from five hudnred years ago would make of all this, or even one of my more primitive European ancestors from the same time, if they had been forced into seeing the future. What could they make of it? "Whew, Bob, did I get into some bad venison last night, or what? You would *not* believe the nightmare I had; in fact, I don't want to tell you about it, or even think about it. It was bad, all of it. Let's go find a new breeze on that other hill."

We are the breeze, in our huge-huge air-conditioned bus, as we twist into Port la Porte, near Galveston. We are here – just up for a cruise, or what?

\*   \*   \*

Sarah has told me, when she called from a sidewalk payphone while she was ashore in Cozumel, Mexico, last week, that she is on greeting duty the day we arrive and so can't meet us at the bus terminal. (J has advised me to not tease Sarah about her greeting outfit. I am, it appears, the type of father who needs to be advised to be sensitive, to not tease about tender spots. I agree with Jan, I am that type of father, more shame to me.) Ben and I follow the bus crowd from inside the dark and high-ceilinged cavern of a terminal, moving out toward the heat and the ship. As we emerge from the building we understand why the line has been moving so slowly, as we are stopped to have our picture taken. When we claim it, later and for a price from the capitalistic photographers, we look tired, hot, pinched, and pale. Immediately in front of us is a long covered gangway, and to the right of that is the massive white ship, spectacular, leashed but ready to go. We feel tiny, and alien.

Sarah sees us coming up the sloping gangway to the entry on Deck 4, and she comes over fast and hugs me long and hard. We haven't seen each other in too long. I glance at her outfit, not saying a word, thinking of it as an ordinary peacock with feathers in the back and a high-cut bottom part, as peacocks sometimes have. I've missed Sarah and it is good to see her, the grin and the eyes, the alert energy and intelligence. She skips out of her greeting work and shows us around the ship. People say hi to her, smiling real smiles. She's at home here.

I, on the other hand, am not at home, and I'm overwhelmed by the multiple incomprehensible stimuli of the ship and from seeing Sarah, by the crowd awash in southern American accents, and by the heavy heat. I'm in need of a truce or a rapid rabbit-hole elevator going down.

Sarah makes shy-mock of her high-cut outfit, saying in a low voice, "Welcome to the ship. How do you like my ass? Have a wonderful week." I probably lose points in some paternalistic deity's eyes because I laugh in appreciation of her humour, and I also think she looks just fine, thank you, ass and all. I keep this opinion to myself. A slim young handsome man, walking by later in shared crowds, says, "Was that your daughter? I was hoping *everybody* got met like that. You got some good-looking daughter, mister," and he grins and gives my arm a pat as he moves on. I smile back, no offense intended or taken. We're all worldly people on this cruise. I'm still cherishing the intense firmness of the greeter's hug.

✳  ✳  ✳

Sarah has arranged a cabin for us at a cheaper rate, on the third level down and in the middle of the ship, aft mid-ship. We are in Cabin #3193 on the Atlantic Deck, and it amazes me how quickly one can feel at home by the simple maneuver of closing the door behind oneself. There are no windows in the cabin, which gives privacy, and it is air-conditioned cool and not too bright with everything having a precise spot and function. It is a comfortable place. I'm desperate to get grounded before being at sea, so while we're still in dock I try to get the mobile overview of the ship implanted and memorized. I start to get a feeling of the possibility of ritual:

- I soon find where the dining areas are, and the casino and lounges, the shops and small library, the deck chairs and swimming pools and walking/jogging route, and even an on-deck basketball hoop. Very soon, in the afternoon, the ship eases out of the berth at Port la Porte, and we lean on the highest railing to watch a long bridge in the background fade into our aft past.

- There is a *Cruise News* available, welcoming us aboard, and suggesting a casual attire. It lists the staff, tells of official sunrise and sunset times (7:09 a.m. and 7:11 p.m.), gives an hour-by-hour list of events of the day, instructs on use of vacuum toilets, encourages us to "protect our oceans" and to "be aware of the ecological balance that must be maintained," gives the assigned seating times and tables for the dining rooms but balances this with an "alternative dining" option at Le Bistro, which is open every night and where "reservations are not required." Ben and I exchange "that is us" looks as we spot Le Bistro.

• We have been told there is an emergency fire and lifeboat drill for 3:30 p.m., soon after we've pulled away from the USA, and the *Cruise News* uses bold font to get us to this "**Mandatory Drill.**" We go. The drill goes well, as not one person is lost at sea during this practice at coping with disaster.

• We go to dinner with Sarah in Le Bistro, and I'm nervous and brittle but manage to not ruin anything important. The staff knows Sarah, speaking to her instantly and with warmth. She is a dancer, a person they know. This gets us linked to the maitre d' and to the server, and also gets me to lighten the hell up. The wine doesn't hurt, either.

• I feel that I'm somehow and very deeply letting down the 1960s side by being on a cruise ship, but the fact that my daughter is working here would have let me off that particularly psychic hook if only I weren't enjoying myself so much. I vow to deal with this betrayal of The Grateful Dead as soon as I get back to Kenora, or much later.

• I amble the decks after dark, looking for positions of comfort, nooks of solitude, trying to get familiar *fast*, trying to cheat, elated and exhausted.

✳  ✳  ✳

I'm awake at 5 a.m., having slept the internally programmed and apparently inflexible six hours, so I get up and start wandering. We're twelve hours south of Texas in the Gulf of Mexico, and I'm feeling very much in need of an anchor, so I go looking. If you don't look, you don't find. There's nobody in the Main Deck rotunda area except for the cleaning staff, and up on the ninth-deck coffee shop there are only a handful of insomniacs, a few solitary cigarette puffers nursing their lonely death wish, and more early-morning staff. I get my two coffees in hand and go back down to the sixth deck, the jogging and walking deck.

The forward part of the ship is kept very dark, possibly to make peering into the night from the ship's bridge on the eighth deck a more effective visual experience, radar or no radar. We're still in full night, with a few clouds and a sliver of moon horizontal to the ocean, an eyeless grin of a moon fragment. It's a clear night and there's no light pollution out here, so I can see the rest of the moon above the sliver, connected but different, gray and obscure but clearly there.

The stars are bright, a full swarm of them, as bright and thick to the eye as from Populus Lake, Ontario, or Bay Chimo, Northwest Territories, that last one about fifteen years ago, then also happily lost to the interfering lights of others. We sail into the end of the night, with the moon remnant shining on the Gulf of Mexico as we occasionally pass a well-lit oil rig in the distance. There are several of these.

I lean on the railing of the sixth deck, nursing left-hand and right-hand coffees, a two-fisted drinker, and watch the ship fold night water under itself. The very forward nose of the ship, just below me on the fifth deck, is the crew's small circular two-metre deep pool and the small bare sunning area. The crew isn't permitted on the top decks, not unless they have visitors and get a special pass, so this week Sarah will be able to visit with us on decks nine and ten. I look down at the empty crew's pool and think about how much and how quickly our lives, mine and my daughters', are moving in different directions. We sail by more oilrigs, well away from us, and the stars and the night fade into day. We have created an improbable space for ourselves in this world.

∗  ∗  ∗

*T*he Franco-Spanish singer-songwriter Manu Chao, who writes and sings in six languages, is declared in a magazine profile to have a "nagging melancholy" and is quoted as having said, "The more I travel, the sadder I get." I know what he means, in that it is somewhat easier to ignore widespread global desperation when you're in your own opaque and stationary shell, but my problem is the opposite of his. The nagging melancholy gets worse for me when I'm stationary, not when I'm mobile. This sea trip, for instance, seems to me to be the ideal time to sort out several issues: how to cope with the increasing physical separation from my daughters, whether or not there is any conceivable justification for cruise ships in a world where an ecological balance must be maintained (as soon as it is rediscovered), how to find solitude on ten decks of crowded no-exit luxury, how to be a less intrusive parent and friend, and whether or not I can ever walk off the increasing limp and weakness which is hanging out in my right arm and leg. There is no possibility, none, that I'm over-reaching here, because this is a full-week sea cruise, after all, a piece of floating cake, icing and all.

Jan has also recently visited Sarah on this ship, and she has set a difficult family precedent. I'm told that J-person played bingo, and won, joined in every activity known to cruisers, including early morning deck walking led by a fitness guy, was excellent at late-night lounge crawling and dancing, and that she was also the most energetic, infectious applauder at the singing and dancing evening entertainments. I'm intimidated, knowing that I cannot measure up to this level of social enthusiasm and expertise, not by a wide margin. I'll be lucky to avoid leaping from the tenth deck railing into the Gulf, screaming some version of "I want to be alone." About day five is when I expect the Captain to have to handcuff me to an anchored-post amidship, well away from any deep or potent liquids.

Instead of leaping I read the day's *Cruise News*. We're on the water all day today, and the *News* actually uses the phrase "At Sea," which tickles my ironic fancy. Sunrise was at 6:58 a.m., and sunset will happen at 6:47 p.m., as we sail toward the equator. Our suggested attire for the day is "Formal," and I'm going to go through the day on the assumption that they mean this attire to be for dinner only. The *News* lists the day's "top activities," including 7 a.m. and 4 p.m. fitness walks, a presentation on ports-of-call in Mexico, an art auction, a Captain's welcome party, gambling tournaments in the Casino, dance classes, ice carving demonstrations, cooking classes, a free consultation on how to avoid bad hair days, Scrabble games, Spanish lessons, Dive In instruction on snorkeling, a Craft Corner instruction session on the making of paper gift boxes, more fitness activities and more gambling (different sites, types and times), a jewelry seminar, a military social, Informal Bridge Play (I reluctantly assume that this refers to the card game, and not to the Captain's site), and liquor tasting in the early afternoon followed by wine tasting in the late afternoon.

The "Friends of Bill W. meet" at 3 p.m. in Gatsby's, Deck 10, Aft, and even though I don't know a single Bill W., I do like the sound of that meeting. I can see a time ahead when "the friends of Pete meet," preferably not in Gatsby's though, but more appropriately at Lyle's trapper cabin in mid-northwestern Ontario, at Whale Cove on Grand Manan Island, and at Halls Harbour in Nova Scotia. Hell, they could have a grand wandering wake of a time, the few friends of Pete, just so long as I stay out of the way.

Ben and I have both been fearful of being organized and hounded into group activity, but we are surprised and delighted to find that other than listing this stupefying mélange of activity choices the *M/S Norwegian Sea* staff leave us well and completely alone. This has the unanticipated (to us) effect of getting us to relax and even join a few things. For example, we go to the Sun-Up Fitness Walk on Deck 6, at 7 a.m., with our Sports Afloat Coordinator Bob. He is not young, and (I'm avoiding use of the agist word "but") he is tanned, trim, handsome, and not annoyingly affable, in fact has a definite edginess in place. Since I'm a secure and sensitive twenty-first-century person, I decide to not instantly hate Bob, and this is a wise choice. After about thirty of us circle the deck in warm, clear sun for forty-five minutes and then do the stop, stretch and relax thing at the end, Ben and I get introduced to Bob. He does a double take, after having been initially quite cool, and asks if I'm Sarah's father, and Jan's too. I confirm yes on both counts, an absolute dad. He looks me in the eye and says I should be very proud of my daughters, as they are wonderful people. I agree, again on both counts, and silently decide that maybe being tanned and aloof and trim doesn't eliminate good judgment. I may even get up at 6:45 a.m. every morning to walk around the deck with this particular Sports Afloat Coordinator.

Later in the morning, after a disciplined low-calorie high-fiber breakfast at the Big Apple Café on Deck 9, where you get to eat outside in a shaded section if you play your cards right, and we do, we go to a lecture by Dr. James Lester, called "Oh My God!! [sic the double exclamations] How Cortez Tricked Montezuma." This is ok, not bad, but I could do better, no question, given a dab or two of research and some preparatory sleep, some more praise for my daughters from Bob, and a microphone that wanders so as to cope with the vacuous acoustics of the Stardust Lounge on Deck 5, aft. I could do much better. This judgmental whimsy leads to a fantasy that begins here and goes on all week, in which I get to work on cruise ships and do lectures that give people both laughter and enlightenment, have my own room, get to see the Caribbean, the Southern US, Mexico *and* the Panama Canal, just as Sarah has. I may even walk every morning, around and around on the fitness deck, before my scintillating talk, so I too will be abdominally trim.

* * *

In my listing of the ship's activities, I didn't mention the two most important ones, a Fashion Show at 3 p.m. and the *Broadway* review at 8:45 and 10:30 p.m. Sarah will be in both of these. I have to coax to get permission to attend the fashion show, so I do coax and do get permission. She is wonderful, with the fifty or so people in the Lounge rising to their feet in a standard Stardust standing-O every time Sarah comes out to the tiny runway area. I wonder where she got the moves, the turns and calm display techniques, and how she has been able to avoid the obligatory arrogance of the Fashion TV shows. She displays clothes *and* warmth, in a way that shows them not to be in opposition. "I'll be damned," I say to Ben, and I mean it.

✳  ✳  ✳

*T*he doors to the stage show *Broadway* open forty minutes before the first show, but Sarah has us go to a corridor away from the main doors where she meets us an hour before the show and walks us through the backstage to the seats. We're introduced to her fellow performers and bosses and the sound/lighting people. We are both nervous, Sarah and I, but Ben is calm. The stage is small and low, with tiny wings, and the seats are spread out in a fan, soft bench seats in a gently rising tier. We wander about, looking for the best vantage point, and select the third row in the center.

I've watched Sarah and Jan dance many times, and I'll never get used to the intensity and the skill required. This week, on this floating stage, Sarah will be in three different shows, Monday, Thursday and Friday evenings, two shows per night, each about an hour in length. She is part of a dance company, the Jean Ann Ryan Company, auditioned for during her final year of Theatre-Dance at Ryerson University in Toronto. As Ben and I sit in the empty lounge, waiting for the doors to open, this moment seems momentous, final in some way. I've been doing this since they were seven years old, hundreds of times, and I'm aware that the aim (one of the aims,

*Suspended – Pete Sarsfield*

anyway) has always been to make a living at it, to be a professional dancer, an entertainer. I always get nervous before they perform and then relax as they hit the stage, as they actually move to the ideas and the music. Benita reaches over to give my arm an it'll-be-ok pat, and then lets me deal with the nerves in my own way. I manage this by recalling my solo and unscheduled pre-registration drop-in meeting with Nadia Potts, the head of Ryerson's program and herself a former major-league dancer, a lead ballerina. Ms. Potts allowed herself to be interrogated regarding her suitability to influence a much-loved daughter, and she did this with careful depth and humour. "If she wants to be a performer, to dance for her living, then this is the place for her," she said, with eye contact and a smile. I think about this as I watch the show, not able to match Jan's precedent setting applause, but not holding back either.

At the end of the second show, getting close to midnight by now, I lean over to the stranger sitting to my left on the bench seat and say, as I point, "That's my daughter, the one there."

✳   ✳   ✳

We had decided before getting here to adopt staying-in-control behaviour: no use of the elevator for the entire week; avoid the assigned dining-rooms with the assigned times and assigned table-mates; don't eat too much and don't drink too much and (there was some thoughtful debate regarding this one) don't think too much; enjoy the days in a relaxed way and don't make having fun be a frantic and ritualistic race against one's inner self; exercise every day; watch and remember the ocean we are fortunate enough to be drifting over; be kind and careful with one's loved ones; and avoid sunburn. Several of these we break, some gladly and some reluctantly, but some are honoured every day.

One of the most enjoyable times we have is the evening meal in Le Bistro, Deck 10, aft, which is open every night from 6 p.m. to midnight. Sarah is able to join us on several evenings, with her

*108*

friend Matt, and her roommate comes over and talks. The maitre d' sits down to chat with us, because of the connection to Sarah, and we learn that he is from Europe and hopes to start a restaurant in Houston. He is tall, thin, shy, smart, and attentive to the needs of the diners. We will go to his restaurant in Houston, if we are lucky. We also have the same server every evening, a man earning a "good living" by living away from his family in Central America. We admire him and are sorry for him, the usual convoluted mixture. The mixture quickly includes affection, as we enjoy the personal and impersonal ritualistic exchange of food, service, respect, and money.

Sometimes we eat early, if we are going to watch Sarah dance, and sometimes we eat late, and always just outside the dining room's large windows is the ocean, a welcome and familiar and potentially lethal saltwater friend. We feel very much at home while cruising at sea, and this surprises both of us.

\* \* \*

Norwegian bills this trip as their Texaribbean Cruise, leaving from Texas and going to the Yucatan Peninsula of Mexico, stopping for a day each in Cancun and Cozumel, then on to the Bay Islands of Honduras where we will stop at Roatan for a day. I figure there's a fairly even split between shore and sea. My allegiances are to the sea, but I'm keen to see both Mexico and Honduras, even a glimpse. Many of Sarah's phone calls, emails, gifts, and letters over the last year have been from Cancun or Cozumel, and the colourful woven friendship bracelet on my right wrist is from there. In addition, on my dining room wall at home in Kenora is a large woven rug brought back by Jan from the west coast of Mexico, the other side. I'm ready for this new country.

The *Cruise News* for Tuesday suggests Texaribbean attire but neglects to give specific details. It must be assumed that we'll just know what this requires, and as most of the ship's passengers are Americans, we'll probably get some helpful hints through subtle Canadian observation as the day unfolds. I've noticed that the ever-helpful *News* always neglects to give weather details or forecasts, never a word. We get extensive lists of the bar specials of the day, wake-up call options and meal hours at all hours, but no weather. I wonder if this might have something to do with the fact that it is hotter than the backside of hell, and much more humid than any prediction of hell I ever heard from the sadistic clergy of my youth, and that we are leaning into the hurricane season, but then I sweep these suspicions under the poolside table as I reach for the Margarita Of The Day, flavour yet to be discovered.

The *News* also gives details about the Yucatan Peninsula, and Cancun in particular, and we are also told of tours available to us when the ship is in port on Tuesday in Cancun, Wednesday in Cozumel, and Thursday in Honduras. Idle hands and empty hearts are the devil's delight, or some such, so there are many tour choices available for each of the three docked days. I'd rather be at sea, being more used to that location, but I keep this sentiment firmly locked in privacy.

Sarah, Ben and I sign up to visit the Mayan ruins at the seaside site of Tulum. The Shore Excursion Desk on Deck 4 advertises this tour as "educational," while some other shore activities listed just below Tulum are billed as "educational, but still fun." Who could ever resist that famous Yankee sales panache? Not us, that's for damn sure, and we sign up for the 6.5-hour trip to Tulum, well-educated diehards to the end. We expect to be alone on this trip.

Ben has been reading a book about Mayan history and is intrigued, leading to a tough choice in tour options. We could be going to Chichen Itza, in fact we think we *should* be going there, as even the tour description handout states that Chichen Itza and the Pyramid of Kulkulcan are "a spectacular once-in-a-lifetime opportunity . . . the largest and most fascinating example of Mayan civilization in the world." The problem is that the two-hour tour of the ruins is bracketed by four and a half hours of ferry and bus ride, nine hours of travelling in total for two hours of educational fun. We decline.

We drop anchor in Cancun harbour at around noon, and to get to the bus that will take us to Tulum an hour and a half south, we are ferried ashore in small boats, as the harbour is too shallow to let our ship dock. I'm told that there's only a couple of metres between our hull and the harbour bottom, and I'm also told that we are going to and from the shore in double-decker ferries called tenders. I'm told these things when I ask questions, a character trait that is met with varying degrees of enthusiasm. I've got to look up "tender" in my dictionary at home in Kenora, as the complete disconnection of meanings is in need of thought and is certain fertile ground for more questions. (It's a living.)

My predictions of an anti-education and/or pro-fun boycott of this trip is proven to be false, as three large buses fill with cruisers keen on education. Our tour guide is Mayan, with a classic (so we are told) Mayan physique and facial features, and a sharp sly sense of humour. We are thick with sticky heat, and our guide doesn't give it a verbal rest for very long. The man sitting immediately in front of us has Tourette's Syndrome, complete with a panoply of involuntary jerks and sounds. We are acutely aware that we have signed on for 4.5 hours of this enclosed shared travelling bliss, for a total of two hours of being herded around some ruins. I'm feeling guilty at having dragged Sarah on this trip when (I suspect) she would prefer to be doing laundry or writing a how's-it-going-after-all-this-time note to her grade three teacher, anything but this. However, we manage to have a good time, and a thoughtful time. The ruins are beside the ocean, enclosed by the remains of a wall, with many stone buildings semi-intact, and with many questions available regarding the why, what, and how. It's a Zen battle to contain myself, a definite growth opportunity.

As we wander the ruins, some as part of the group and some of it on our own, I'm again struck by the thought I had at 6 a.m. while perched at the bow of the *M/S Norwegian Sea*. We have created an improbable space for our species on this planet. These people, the Mayans, established a protected, dominating and elite niche for themselves, with significant effort and skill and the usual allocation of brutality. Their "classic period" is stated to have been between 250 and 900 A.D., after which they gradually (and predictably) outgrew their food supply and other necessities, and maybe their very reason for existence. We dig our own traps, and we do so with such flair. I recently received a postcard from a friend who was visiting Iceland, in which he says, ". . . its culture is sophisticated . . . but raison d'etre a mystery."

\*   \*   \*

We leave Cancun at about 10 p.m. and sail all night, getting to the dock in Cozumel at 6 a.m. I'm up early to watch the docking and to read the *Cruise News* for the day ahead. The name Cozumel comes from the Mayan name Ah-Cuzamil-Peten, or Island of the Swallows, a sacred fertility shrine visited by each Mayan woman "at least once during her lifetime." I watch the ship ease into the dock, angled parallel to the shore, and I'm enjoying myself a great deal, feeling fertile. We don't want to do any tours today, and Sarah is going to take us shopping, as she knows the town well, then she and Matt are taking us to a tiny quiet beach they have found.

We shop and buy rings, wine glasses and wall hangings, then we swim and sun and talk and drink beer. I miss the ship, the movement of it, but not that much. This is a relaxed day, one for the serenity bank. We leave at 5 p.m., sailing for the Bay Islands of Honduras.

\*   \*   \*

The ship's TV, in cabin #3193 on the Atlantic Deck, has several channels: one with news and one with sports, several with consumer-exhortation advice, and one of movies. Glancing at John Wayne I'm reminded of Texan Lyle Lovett's song about riding his pony on his boat, a lasting image, possibly beyond even the Duke's talents.

There are two other channels on the tiny TV. One is a simple link to a camera on the ship's bridge, giving a straight-ahead view of where we're going. At night the screen is dark, as we sail straight ahead into darkness. The other is educational, which reaffirms my conviction that Norwegian is in business to teach, with fun and profit as loss leaders. This educational channel has a recurring multi-part documentary on dinosaurs. They, too, the script goes, became more and more improbable. I spend some time watching the computer-generated extinct reptiles, escaping in my own way from the heat of the sun and the proximity of so many people, perched on the edge of my cot in Cabin #3193's air-conditioned ease, ignoring all easy ironies.

*  *  *

*I* definitely need to get out more, as I've never heard of Honduras' Bay Islands. The *Cruise News* for Thursday, picked up on my early morning solitude and coffee run, gives details:

> "LAS ISLAS DE LA BAHIA – You may recognize the travel destination as the Bay Islands, which consist of eight islands and more than 60 bays, that are collectively known as Las Islas de la Bahia. These islands rest upon the Bonacca Ridge, the result of an enormous crack that runs along the ocean floor, about 40 miles northeast of the north coast of Honduras . . . The largest of the eight islands is Roatan, which is 40 miles long and less than 4 miles wide at its widest point. The people of Roatan, population 30,000, have ancestral origins from eight separate cultures: English, Spanish, Pavan Indians, Afro-Antillean, Anglo-Antillean, Spanish Honduran and North American."

Las Islas de la Bahia – I like the sound of that, and I also like the writing style of the *Cruise News* author(s). I make a mental note, number forty-eight, to claim to be able to do this, when I try to sell myself for future cruise ship worker status.

The suggested attire for the day is '50's and '60's styles, and I am so pleased that I brought my customary seven suitcases along on this trip, to cope with all the necessary changes. The *News* also tells of the evening's entertainment plan, as they are "proud to present the Tony Award Broadway Musical *Grease*" at 7 and 9 p.m. I'm probably the only human off the northeast coast of Honduras who has never seen *Grease* in any form, not the movie or the play, not the TV show, and I have not read the book, but I'm undaunted. Sarah is in this and will again bring us in the back door before both shows, so before the night is over I'll know the story, at least my daughter's part of it.

We dock at Rotan's largest community of Coxen Hole at about 10 a.m., near the popular artistic shops called Shepherd's Lot and Yaba Ding Ding, as the local map and information sheet informs us. I like the look of this place, as it appears to be a true community and not an appendage to tourism's wallet. We've signed up for another shore excursion, and we're getting smarter. This time we're on the bus for only forty minutes each way, to Tabyana Beach on the West End of the island via Panoramic Road, and the road's name is accurate. The bus driver stops at the peak of the muddy twisting steep hill to allow us a view of trees and ocean, coves and folding hills, and it is a wise stop. This is a beautiful place. Ben and I exchange glances and one-line coded agreements – we'll be back here, the gods and credit cards permitting.

Tabyana Beach is crowded and scenic, with deck chairs in the scorching sun or to be dragged under palm trees. Many people have signed up for snorkeling lessons while others are being taken out in glass-bottomed boats to see the coral reefs, "the world's second largest barrier reef that offers the most spectacular diving and snorkeling in the Western Caribbean." Near to where we're seated, watching the world evolve around us, there is a large sign that says, "Por Favor No Tocar O Pararse En El Coral," or "Please Do Not Touch Or Stand On The Coral." Apparently, the Roatanians have problems with pararses, as do we all.

As the afternoon moves along, the sky clouds over and then darkens to an ominous depth, complete with wind coming up strong and waves increasing. Ben and I have gone for a walk along the beach, to escape people and look for sights and because the little map we've been given lists the Inn of Last Resort just up along. As we get not very far on the beach, however, nowhere near any resort, last or otherwise, the sky becomes deeply dark and starts to bang out thunder, lightning and monsoon sheets of slashing rain. Someone has pissed off the sky gods to an extreme degree, and even though we didn't do it, whatever it was, we shouldn't be out here. This is dangerous. We approach a private-looking building, knock on the door, get no answer, and then spend about thirty minutes avoiding doom by standing pressed back to the wall under someone's overhanging roof. We get wet, but that's all, and it is fun to watch. Scary fun is the best kind of fun, sometimes.

On the bus back to the ship we sit near two people from Texas. We've noticed that most of the ship's passengers are Texans, and we're enjoying watching the mating, drinking, and conversational rituals of this exotic species. These folk make Newfoundlanders seem boring. The two bus-mates are smart and tough, not shy, and they call each other "Honey" all the time. The man speaks Spanish to the bus driver, and he has a collection of tattoos that again makes me want to get body- decorated. They seem to recognize us as a foreign species, slow moving and afraid of any quick movements or loud noises. They treat us with the Texan equivalent of kid gloves, which means that we are not required to burst into a spontaneous rendition of the lone star anthem nor do we have to share body-part details or marital histories. Mr. and Mrs. Honey, as Ben names them, sit near us for dinner later this day in Le Bistro, and we talk back and forth across the table gaps, they being more subdued and we more animated in this (our) more familiar turf.

We seem to have blundered into a parallel reversed universe where at some point in the day we'll have to stand up to declare "Hi, I'm Pete, and I'm not a Texan, nor do I want to be one," or (and this is my more cherished vision) in a startled voice do our Academy Award reversal, saying, "I can't believe this, but we like you, we really *LIKE* you!" There is simply no accounting for the flux of circumstances.

\* \* \*

We've also been able to observe the strange racial adjustment Americans make, or to be fair and to narrow it to the perceived reality of our one tiny floating week, specifically the adjustments made by a few observed Americans on the *M/S Norwegian Sea* for this week in September. There are many black and white Americans on this cruise, the majority being Texans. The accommodation they seem to make toward each other is one of careful and unrelenting non-acknowledgement. We see many walk-bys and other proximities of blacks and whites without a flicker of eye contact or other recognition, nothing. Blacks meeting blacks or whites meeting whites, however, seem to have a wide array of friendly, semi-friendly, cool, or non-existent recognitions, the whole gamut, as you'd expect.

On several occasions, being Canadian and, therefore, more ignorant of racial etiquette, we hold a door for blacks coming close behind us, and we occasionally nod and smile, and on a couple of late-evening or early-morning encounters when it isn't crowded, we even speak. The response to our naïve gaffes are themselves instructive, ranging from a cool and dismissive glance to a startled yet friendly response to match our lead, and more rarely a complete ignoring of our very existence. We have a lot to learn from the Americans, and I'm surprised and grateful that they haven't added a charge for this. "Don't be too sure, until we see the final bill," says Ben, when I share my impressions.

*　*　*

This is Sarah's second cruiseship job, and on mail sent to her on the first one, the *Regal Empress*, it eased delivery if JAR/Entertainer was added after her name, JAR for Jean Ann Ryan Dance Company, and Entertainer for just that. While I enjoyed writing that down, every time, I don't appreciate its significance until I watch Sarah shine as the good-hearted airhead Frenchy in *Grease*, constantly grinning and fluffing her hair and adjusting her breasts upwards, in character without waver two weeks post injured leg and in the midst of continuing pain. She *is* an entertainer, and the crowd loves her – me, too.

The next night, Friday evening, the shows are at 9 and 10:45 p.m., and the production is *Sea Legs Express*, a demanding medley celebrating the ports touched by cruise ships around the world. We've been "at sea" all day, as noted by the *Cruise News*, and the weather has been stormy, windy from the forward edge of a brewing tropical storm, with rain and dark skies. Even with the stabilizers in place the ship is moving around, and I'm surprised that the performance won't be cancelled. Sarah gets us seated early, before the peasants who don't have dancing daughters, and this involves our carefully holding on to the seats as we lurch to a central spot in the third row. The show is a non-stop high-energy burst of fast and intricate jazz steps, now timed so that the heaving ship doesn't toss a dancer or two into the eighth row. I don't know how they do it, but they do, and no one is injured or makes an ass of themselves, the order of importance of these risks varying with your parental or dancer status.

Sitting to my left, and the Cabaret Lounge is packed tonight so we're in close contact on this bench seat, is a woman who appears to be (at my guess) from the Philippines, and to her left is her husband, a white Texan. The woman and I chat a bit, and she is able to find out that my daughter is dancing. She wrings it out of me. I begin to tell her which one is Sarah, but she quickly says, "Don't tell me" before I have pointed or said anything descriptive, adding, "I want to see." She watches the dancers carefully, ignoring my eyes and interest, just focusing on the stage. After a while she leans to me and says, "There is your daughter. She's very good," and she is right.

After *Sea Legs*, the company comes out on stage to meet any of the audience who want to talk. I hang back to watch, a constant believer in free theatre. A young girl, four or five years old, approaches Sarah, with her parents also hanging back a step, supportive and present but letting her do this on her own, more or less. Sarah bends down to be at the girl's level, even though it isn't easy in the tight costume. The girl wants to meet Sarah and she wants to be a dancer. They talk for a few minutes, and the girl seems pleased that she is being treated seriously and with warmth. She can't take her eyes off Sarah's face. Sarah looks up and sees me watching, and she sees the look on my face. She smiles at me.

✳ ✳ ✳

We're at sea all day Friday and Saturday, outrunning and outflanking the edge of the storm, and the *Cruise News* for these two days reflects this winding-down status, emphasizing that we are "homeward bound," and scheduling a "final blowout art auction" and a "final jackpot bingo" as well as a one-hour "debarkation briefing," for those who worry about such things. Ben and I have our own final not-to-be-missed list, and we get right to it on these at sea days.

We've skipped the previous ship's bridge tour, so we make this last one, being shown around by Captain Idar Hoydal and his officers, most of whom are indeed Norwegian. We learn that this ship was built in Finland in 1988, is 709 feet long, or 216.35 metres for the Euro-Canadians amongst the crowd, and it has a maximum speed of 25.9 miles per hour. They tell us much detail about engines, propellers, bow thrusters, stabilizers, the power plant, evaporators, steering gear, fuel consumption, the air conditioning plant, and an unending amount of verbiage about the navigational equipment. I ignore it all, boring, boring, deadly boring. Some of the more comprehensible details gather a touch of life, however, such as the fact that there are 21 officers and 630 crew for 1,800 passengers and that the "stopping distance" is 3.6 minutes or 0.33 nautical miles "from full ahead." There are 258 fire hydrants, 9 passenger decks, 18 public rooms, and 3 swimming pools on the *M/S Norwegian Sea*. The distance from Houston to Cancun is 700 nautical miles, while from Cancun to Cozumel is only 50 nautical miles, Cozumel to Roatan is 175 n. miles, and this return dark-sky sojourn from Roatan to Houston will be 1,000 n. miles. I feel heavy with fact as we leave the bridge on the near edge of enlightened.

Ben and I have had our full-dress pictures taken by the photographic wizards, and this was an annoying process, as they felt obliged to pose us as they saw fit rather than as we wished to be seen and were openly dismissive when we declined to buy into their pseudo-artistic stereotypically role-rigid and cloying version of coupledom. This became colder but bearable when I stated my intention to walk, depart with wallet zipped, unless they took our direction as well as our money. The picture we have from this entrepreneurial encounter is adequate, attractive in a sculpted-ice way, but my favourite photo of the week is one Sarah took of us in the marble-lined entry to the Cabaret Lounge, before the crowd came in. We look happy, relaxed, tanned, well-dressed, and in the presence of a friend.

\* \* \*

*Suspended – Pete Sarsfield*

We aim toward Houston early on Sunday, and I'm thankful to the *Cruise News* for the information regarding luggage preparation, tipping, customs and immigration, settling of accounts, and the timing and destination of airport buses. I mean this gratitude, I'm being sincere. Departure is a daunting process, almost as bad as arrival.

To be specific, I don't want to leave Sarah, but am becoming more aware of the necessity of doing so. She has shown me a lot this week, about dancing and the state of her heart, and about the difficulties and benefits of mobility. I'm pleased for her that she has done this, and I'm pleased for her that she won't do much more of it. It is a lonely and exciting and superficial way to make a living. The superficiality appeals to me, but I'll have to think about that, about why it appeals. I might try it for a while, in years to come, but I'll have to get Sarah's advice first.

The *Norwegian Sea* docks, and we leave.

*M/S Norwegian Sea, Gulf of Mexico*
*Cozumel, Mexico*
*Roatan, Honduras*

# *Caught in Winter*

*I*t's 7:30 a.m., dark in January, and I'm late starting out from
Kenora for the three-hour drive to Sioux Lookout, having gone
first into the office to do email. It's an icy-road day, with Thunder Bay's CBC radio early-morning program suggesting that we
find some reason to phone-in as a no-show, grab a book, light the
fireplace and listen to CBC all morning: "It doesn't matter; just stay
off the roads." I decide to ignore all this and give it a try.

The OPP officer at the top of the first hill, near where the Trans
Canada bypass joins the Kenora road, has a different opinion, telling
me the highway is "closed all the way to Ignace," so go on back and
relax, grab a book, light a fire, the whole chant. I thank him and
turn back, but once I'm out of sight, I cut left onto a side road and
do a couple of jigs, coming out on the Trans Canada, highway #17,
now on the other side of the cop.

I'm quite proud of myself and settle back to a careful speed, a
paranoid one as I am aware that I've hoisted my middle finger *and*
thumbed my nose at both the ice gods and the OPP. I have very little
room for error.

It *is* slippery, no argument, all the way to Vermilion Bay, but I
get there in only two hours, about twice the usual time. At the junction of the Trans Canada and the turnoff to Ear Falls and Red Lake,

another OPP officer is perched, lights flashing on her car, freezing rain and snow blowing around her. She says I'm here in Vermilion Bay for a while, quite a long while, as "the roads are closed every which way." (There is no side road.)

I go back a mile or so to Buster's, the restaurant I've been in for more on-the-road meals than any other in the region. It's got stuffed fish and animal heads on the walls, and I hate death and decapitations on walls, and it's also got cigarette smoke and non-stop country music on a high-mounted TV, and I deeply dislike smokey country, and yet I like Buster's, a lot. Priorities are important; they balance things. The owners and staff are friendly straight-eye gazers, and they know my name. The soups are excellent, thick with vegetables and flavour and salt, as are the sandwiches, and the chairs are familiar and comfortable. On this iced-over day, for instance, I spend over five hours doing paperwork at their table, eating their food but definitely not five hours worth, and the staff and owners are unceasingly relaxed. They don't even mind when Bill phones their business number looking for me, tracking me down from the Kenora office. "I *knew* you'd be there," he grins over the line, as we've shared many road lunches at these tables.

Mid-afternoon, I see the plow go by in a purposeful cloud, moving east towards Dryden, and I gather my papers and stuff to hustle out of Buster's with a plan. I plead my case to the OPP officer, saying that I'll follow the plow to Dryden and then stop for the night. "I wouldn't lie to you," I offer. "Yeah, right!" she says, not even faintly impressed. "Ok, go ahead, but if you go off the road, you're going to sit there for a *long* time."

The ride to Dryden is disconcerting, with several empty cars and trucks in the ditches, so I *do* stop for the night, only an hour away from Sioux Lookout. It's a tie game, between me and the ice demons, and I'll accept the score without complaint. "We played good and they played good, so it's just great that no one had to go home a loser," that's how my inner Sports Report sums up the day.

\* \* \*

122

The next day at about noon I get into Nibinamik First Nation, also called Summer Beaver, following a 9 a.m. departure from Sioux Lookout and wind-bumped snow-blinded stops in Lansdowne House, Fort Hope, and Webequie. Our flight was in a two-engine two-pilot plane, one which could hold about twelve passengers if full, but it wasn't. Small planes avoid the pretense of being a crowded restaurant in the air, but instead force recognition of the fact that we should not be up here. We can feel all too clearly that we could break apart and spill out, or bump into something, or simply cease this attempt at flight and give in to gravity as we merge with the grounded environment. One does not feel immortal in high tumultuous air.

Over the next five days I enjoy a return to my work roots, living in the Nursing Station, finding community art and crafts, meeting Band representatives, watching more television than is healthy, walking around the beautiful and cohesive community, working the phones for both task and affection, doing on-site Public Health and even a bit of ill-health work, and being drawn to blank sheets of paper, over and over. I feel at home, relaxed, in a place where I can watch and think and just let the stimuli flood on in.

The stimuli are thick and rich. Soon after the plane from Sioux Lookout has spat me out onto the Nibinamik airstrip, the weather closes down around the town, wrapping it completely in freezing rain, and then in a blizzard of blowing snow for the rest of the week. I am "stuck," and feeling blessed by this fact as it gives me a chance to mentally and physically hang out in my old-hometown, figuratively speaking.

Just being in a Nursing Station again is a treat. Four of us share the visitors' apartment, four strangers having to adjust to one bathroom, a small kitchen, differing addictions to movie and television violence, thin walls, and wildly variant temperature, volume, solitude, and conversation needs. On one freezing-rain flight-cancelled evening I make a list of Nursing Stations where I've spent a good portion of my adult life, in both senses of the concept of "good." My list reaches fifty names, and it's a nostalgic rush to see the roll-call on paper: from Nain and Davis Inlet, Black Tickle, Mary's Harbour, and Port Hope Simpson in Labrador to Coppermine, Gjoa Haven, Pelly Bay, and Spence Bay in the Kitikmeot Region, from Coral Harbour and Chesterfield Inlet in the Keewatin Region of the (then) NWT to Red Sucker Lake, Bloodvein, Poplar River, and Thicket Portage in Manitoba, and for-now-finally to Muskrat Dam, North Spirit Lake, Nibinamik, and Deer Lake in northern Ontario. I watch the snow-clogged wind folding around the Station and re-member the gifts of time and friendship I've been offered in these places.

Summer Beaver, I am told, was founded in the mid-'70s as a spin-off of the nearby communities. Most of the Anishinaabe residents, and many of the rest of us, now call the community Nibinamik, which translates as "place where beavers are caught in summer," the name of the area long before English words intruded. Nibinamik has about four hundred people, one police officer, several stores, a new school, and a new Nursing Station. All buildings in the town are either made of logs or have log-look exterior siding, such as on the school and Nursing Station.

A forest fire came right up to the edge of town a few years ago, and the town is surrounded by standing dead spruce, now potential firewood. Only one small out-building merged with the dust when the fire lapped up against the town. The standing-dead-wood does not, for some reason, give the place a Mordor-like appearance. In-stead, it seems to add a useful edge of benign starkness, a few wrin-kles of contrast.

I wander the streets, some of it on my own and some with Kevin, the Environmental Health Officer who is orchestrating the visit. As with most of my life, I find that the images approach and connect in random order:

- There is a soft constant scent of wood smoke as I walk around the five interlinking streets. I love this smell, feeling it to be from the heart, connected to the land in a paradoxical and sustainable way. It is entirely possible that this affection is based on a foolish premise. The wood smoke also awakens a fond memory of walking with Rene in North West River and then living at Grand Lake, both places in Labrador, twenty-five years ago, luxuriating in the same wafts of smoke from many other chimneys. Some things change, and some don't.

• In the Band-owned store, where I'm stocking up on easily managed food items for my extra storm-stayed days, a girl of nine or ten comes up to me, to look at my face and to chat, or so it seems. After a few seconds of name exchanges and general pleasantries, she asks for a dollar. I say, "Nope, not a chance," and she loses interest ever so fast. I'm off her cross-cultural pen-pal list.

• The nurse-in-charge, Daisy, and the Community Health Representative (CHR), Jeannie, are sisters and from this community. They are strong, friendly, clever, and skilled. They guide Kevin and me through a problem-solving meeting with Band councilors, and the resulting community-supportive letter. We all compose, edit, and sign the final version and it has a cooperative and useful feel. In comparing stories about our kids, our roles and about health-care, Daisy, Jeannie and I seem to find expanding areas of agreement. My inclination is to ask them to adopt me, but perhaps I'd better wait.

• When I ask what artists I should pursue, I'm directed to Moses Beaver. I call, asking if I can visit to see his work, and he says it'll have to be between 5 and 6 p.m., as he's playing hockey at 2 p.m. and again at 8 p.m. Jeannie shows me how to get to his

house, using the large hand-made map of the community that's on the Nursing Station corridor wall,
to orientate me.

Moses is at home alone, and the fire has gone out in his stove so
the place is chilly. His team won the afternoon game, and his seven-
teen-year-old son is on the opposing team later this evening, so it's a
full day, Hockey Night in Summer Beaver.

He shows me his pen and ink drawings as well as the water-
colours and a couple of oils. He has two drawings of ravens that are
evocative of that bird's complex cleverness, but they are out of my
price range. They are worth every bit of his asking price, but I just
don't have it. However, Moses also lets me look at several of his pre-
liminary working sketches, and is willing to let me buy two of them.
"But they're not finished," he says. "The paper's wrong on that one,
and those marks . . . they're not finished."

I tell him that I like them, and will hang them carefully. We
awkwardly agree on a price and both seem to feel we have an agree-
able deal, which as far as I'm concerned is one of the central aims of
the exercise. Later, I show Daisy and Jeanne the sketches, and they
also like them. "Those are beautiful," Daisy says, and I think she is
particularly fond of the smaller one, which has the heads and bodies
of two geese united in one set of wings, backdropped by a red sun.
Moses Beaver didn't like the choice of paper for this one, but the
problem is too subtle for me. The other drawing, more blatantly un-
finished with pencil-sketch still evident for the yet-to-be-completed
ink overlay, has an osprey hovering above waves, with a fragmented
sun overlooking this survival scene. Moses Beaver has signed both
drawings for me, using his deceased wife's syllabic signature as well
as his own name in English. I hope to see him again.

Kevin and I watch part of a hockey game played on an outdoor
rink, with spectators at the ends behind protective wire screen and
others along the sides sitting on their ski-doos with no protection.

The game is played intently, rough and clean, and I don't see even a hint of a fight.

We then go back to the grocery store, where Kevin inspects, praises and directs while I stay on the periphery. Later, we wander into the police office to say hello to the constable, who is soon to become Chief of Police for a multi-member force on a nearby Reserve. His style is supportive and it would be good if it transplants with ease. I wish him luck and mean it, and he senses my concern, my pessimism about social contracts in general, disarming it and me with a confident grin and saying, "I think I'll be fine."

The Catholic church is a beautiful small structure, made of logs with a thin-post stockade surrounding it, like an old-fashioned made-for-TV fort. No one appears to have taken offense, however, as it is untouched even though empty, with the priest visiting occasionally from Lansdowne House. I'm told that the priest is well liked, possibly accounting for the protected status of the anachronistic building. It all seems to come down to this, again and again; if you're liked, you're somewhat safe. If not, forget it; sell your clothes. In Toronto and Calgary, Kenora and Kentville, Cambridge Bay and Nibinamik, you had better try to be nice, and it's even better if you can mean it. It's no wonder *nice* has such a bad name, what a pain in the vulnerable ass. Of course, there's always the balancing fact that *nice* offers no protection against the bullets and arrows of outrageous fortune, none whatsoever. I suppose this leveling effect of chance should provide some rueful comfort to the huge bunch of us who occasionally veer away from nice.

As always, I've got the random and voluminous flood of images spread out on the table in front of me, like so many pieces of a jigsaw puzzle, but without the helpful photos of the desired completion on the box cover. I have no idea what pattern this or any other flow of images is leading towards, and it doesn't matter, not to me. What *does* matter is allowing the pieces to be seen, and occasionally to even find a few that fit together. "That one, the one over there with the ironic grin, will fit with the hovering osprey, don't you think?"

The wind drops, and the cloud-cover lifts, and the plane which has been cancelled for several days gets dusted off in Sioux Lookout and may come in later, in a few hours. I may get home tonight. Then again, if I am allowed to stay here, I'll feel at home. There is no losing; there is only winning.

*Vermilion Bay, Ontario*
*Nibinamik First Nation*

# The Cormorants' Job

*I*t's Good Friday and I'm a Catholic atheist sitting in a rented and sparsely furnished cabin in Miners Bay village on Mayne Island, Gulf Islands, British Columbia. I'm looking out at late afternoon rain drifting across Active Pass, washing the frequently passing ferries. Gordon Lightfoot is on CBC, caught on the small radio I bought yesterday in West Vancouver, and he's singing "Early Morning Rain." The mood is perfect for Good Friday, and I toast the rain gods.

Watching the ferries crisscross and weave through the narrow Active Pass, I remember another Good Friday, decades ago, when my father was staying at home, deep into his melancholic cups instead of going to the gloomy and tedious mid-afternoon service. He did do his parental duty, however, and sent me off to represent the family at the church, or so he intended. (I can't remember where my sister Sue was in this equation, how she escaped, and I have to admit that she was probably well ahead of me in learning how to hide-out on Good Friday. I better compliment her, and up-the-ante by putting Mayne-Island-in-the-rain into the pot.) In one of those classic nobody-loses-as-long-as-the-truth-is-hidden moves, I left the house at 2:30 for the 3 p.m. service, dressed in solemn duds, walking. I was in my mid-teens. At the bottom of the hill, around the corner, Charlie and Russ were waiting for me, with my hockey bag.

We all mark the deaths of our gods in our own ways, and it is the attitude of observation that counts, not the site. That was my firm opinion as I was enlisted to play nets that day, to be the goalie instead of going to church. This goaltending positioning was due to the absence of anyone else willing to endure the barrage of shots and also due to my lack of ability at *any* position, including nets. At least in goal I could just stand there and provide a partial obstacle. This enlistment was in the pre-mask days of personal protection, but who knew that, then?

Near the end of the afternoon, a guy broke down the wing, coming at me on a partial breakaway, and he wound up for a show-no-mercy slap shot from just inside the blue line. Billy had played some serious hockey elsewhere, and he also took himself very seriously indeed, so my life was in jeopardy as he leaned into the shot. I still don't know how I did what I did, probably a reflex self-protection response, as my left pad kicked out, seemingly of its own will, deflecting the bullet-shot away from the lower corner of the net and off to the boards. The gasps of disbelief from other players were most appropriate to the day, showing awe at that which cannot be comprehended. I accepted having been spared as a sure sign of the divine comedy, a gleeful warning shot, "*Don't* push your luck, idiot child. I've got a bull's-eye taped on your forehead, should I choose to want to hit it, at *any* time."

When I got home for supper, my father asked about the service. I said, "Mortality is *much* too strange for me." As Mom had died at this time of year about five years before and there was also the matter of the marking of Jesus' death that very day, Dad wasn't about to enter a discussion of the topic, which was exactly what I'd counted on. If I'd had a face full of stitches it might have been more difficult to pull off, but events do evolve in mysterious ways, even on Good Fridays.

\*　\*　\*

In Mayne Island's Cabin #2, the glass sliding door has been shattered. In the way of new-age glass, this has not resulted in a collapse, as there has been no falling from the door frame to the floor and deck. Instead, the entire panel of glass is a complex and complete spider-web of intact cracks, a honeycomb, a maze. I touch it, to make sure it is indeed broken-yet-intact and not just someone's idea of decorative sculpting or even a visual safety measure to stop people from walking into the door. The cracks are real, palpable, sharp-edged. I search for a centre to the maze, a pattern, as metaphors are supposed to lead somewhere, if they know what they're up to. This one doesn't, as it's nothing but random cracks leading nowhere. I like this door, and open and close it very carefully.

\*　\*　\*

At night the ferries go through Active Pass more slowly, feeling their cautious way across the angled water path. In the dark of my room I listen to a CBC radio interview with BC poet Lorna Crozier as I watch a huge ferry tip-toe through, with Crozier's wit and warmth acting as a playful dance partner for the ponderous and reticent ship, point and counterpoint, a duet of unequals. Crozier's interview ends and the ferry glides out of sight. My room stays dark.

\*　\*　\*

I had been planning to make my supper but fall asleep on the couch while reading Elmore Leonard. Surely, I've just discovered a new and specific diagnostic test for precipitously falling testosterone levels, falling-asleep-while-reading-Dutch. The acronym can be FARD, eventually leading to an Old Fard ward at the soon to be completed Inactive Pass Home for the Partially Weary. I've got dibs on the room closest to the waves.

I get up from the couch, groggy, and splash water on my face and comb my hair before going out into the lashing rain and wind, aiming for the nearby Saltwater Lodge Dining Room. I'm still in my day-stained jeans and my lime-green DALHOUSIE UNIVERSITY sweat-shirt, with matching seen-better-days leather jacket and duck-boots. My hair is soon no longer combed. Sartorially speaking, I'm prime for a with-all-due-disrespect dining-room service experience, or even to be sent packing into that dark damp night to order a pizza or (worse yet) to warm for myself. The combination host and waiter re-assures me that I look grand, "simply grand," and in her rough-edged smoker's voice, responding to my query about non-smoking areas, tells me that the whole bleeping building is non-smoking, bless the government's pathetic and twisted little heart. By now I'm in love and so I say, "Don't you just *hate* that?" and she responds with warmth and eye contact as she seats me at a small table and leaves me with a melt-my-heart smile, to the mercy of my first-day waiter. I take it as a compliment, indicating that I look kind and not impoverished nor lacking all powers of discrimination.

The nearest table to me has two people, a woman and a man in their sixties, and they've heard the no-smoking-lament exchange. He is displeased at this, in full pissed-off indignant fury that some-one should even *think* of lighting up, because that's how he has in-terpreted my comments, mistaking which hot-burning stick I was promoting. He goes on at loud length about this, to the quietly nod-ding woman he's with. I try to enhance this tiny fire with fresh gaso-line by patting my jacket pockets and saying loudly to myself,

"Where *are* those damned cigars?" The woman companion gets a glint in her eyes, as she suspects downward tugs on her man's leg, but if push comes to puff I'll bet my non-existent Cuban El Supremo that she'll stand by her guy.

I do enjoy my meal, along with a couple of dark beer but no cigars. Life is good for us old fards.

\* \* \*

The Seal Beach area at Miners Bay has a long, functioning wharf, and off to the side, almost directly in front of my windows, are the remnants of another wharf, now deceased. All that's left are five side-by-side sets of upright log pilings with nothing joining them, just poles in the water. In the early morning, cormorants perch on the tops of these poles, one on each, lined up. They give the defunct wharf an attitude. They appear to be watching the morning sun as it begins to light up the end of Galiano Island, just across the water, and as the first BC Ferries of the day come twisting through Active Pass. The cormorants guard the beginning of the day; it's their job.

In closer to the shore from this skeletal pier is a huge log, one end out in deeper water and the other about three metres from water's edge. The strange thing is that the log's deeper end is fixed to the bottom, waterlogged or wedged, while the end nearer to shore bobs with the waves. When a large ferry goes by and the wash reaches shore in a few minutes, the log-end rises and falls with vigour, imitating an indecisive whale. The moss-covered log-head comes up out of the water to view the land, trying to decide whether to feel scorn or envy, or, if it's one smart log, both. The breaching log of Miners Bay, with bets being taken as to which end will prevail. (The betting never stops.)

\* \* \*

Later, I hear a radio piece on another variation of the cormorants' work, and its one that I should thoroughly research before writing of it. The topic demands that, but I don't want to, not this topic and not this writer. The version I recall, and picture my hand poised to smack the radio turn-off switch as you judge the accuracy, has Japanese in-shore small-boat fishers forming partnerships, of a sort, with captive "pet" cormorants. They, the fishing people, tie something around the neck of the bird, so it can't swallow, and then send this skilled diving-bird into the water to bring back a captured fish. Over and over, the bird dives to water as its species always has, catches a fish, and brings it back to the human in the boat. I can't remember if the bird is tied to a retrieval rope, say by its foot, and this is precisely what I should be turning encyclopedic cormorant pages to determine, but I don't have the heart for it.

The reason for my reaction is that at the end of the radio piece it is stated that when the cormorant's fishing days are over (due to osteoarthritis or underwater-speed-slowdown or better new birds in the coop – our usual reasons), instead of letting the bird go, or giving it prized-place at the fishing table, the fisher-person kills the bird. The radio voice says that this is a sad moment for the human killer, or so I remember the script, but a released bird would just be more competition, and one cannot tolerate *that*. Sorry, old trusted fishing partner of mine, but . . . WHAP.

\* \* \*

I walk often, sometimes long walks and sometimes not. On Mayne Island there is one I grow fond of, from the village of Miners Bay up a steep hill and along Georgina Point Road to the lighthouse, where one can sit and watch the rocky beach and waves and boats before starting back. This is a winding tree-lined walk, slightly difficult at the beginning but still just a walk in the woods with a peaceful ocean at the end.

There are several artists on this route, makers of image-filled things, selling glass sculptures and complex textured earrings, shirts and cards, sketches and paintings. They all live near the lighthouse, separately. One talks easily and directly and appears to see the person standing near him, while the blower-of-glass is much more fragile, closed-off and wary, accepting viewers into his brightly intricate space only when he has to, and even then only briefly. I know how they feel.

This lighthouse walk is a sustaining one, and I follow it several times, letting myself learn to fit. On one of the last days of my visit, I have come up the monster hill and am along the twisting road at the top, near the tall spruce, cedar and pine, past the deadend turnoffs of Laura Pond Road and Nell Road with Tinkley and Cotton Roads to come, when I hear a nearby heavy rustle of wings, overhead. I look up, startled, to see an adult bald eagle land on the top of an evergreen, close to the road and close to me. I stand to watch it, until the huge, potent bird decides it has better things to do than be scrutinized by this groundhog, if it has noticed me at all. It flies off, a powerful and relaxed departure. I walk over to the base of the tree, wondering, and there is a large feather lying there. I look at it for a few minutes before picking it up, trying to decide what respect demands, finally deciding to just go with the script as presented. I've lived beside aboriginal people long enough to know that encounters with eagles are to be taken seriously and have obligation attached. The feather carries weight.

For the next couple of days, until I leave, I make sure to wait for someone to offer themselves to me, someone more deserving of this connection, but either this doesn't happen or I don't let myself recognize the person.

I keep the feather, carefully, but kept nevertheless. With some luck and skill, I may find someone to help me interpret why I have been visited, to what purpose. I hope I've got the ability to move my game up a few notches.

\* \* \*

*O*ne year later, Ben and I spend Good Friday and the second day of Passover on Greyhound buses from Winnipeg to Vancouver, and then at 7:30 a.m. grab a cab from downtown to the ferry terminal in Tsawwassen, about forty kilometres southwest of the city. We are bleary-eyed, and lucky, stumbling aboard with five minutes to go before sailing. The *Queen of Tsawwassen* takes a bit over an hour to sail to Village Bay on Mayne Island, with one stop on the way, at Galiano Island. As we ease into the wood-pilings of the ferry-dock at Sturdies Bay on Galiano, we see a bald eagle circling low overhead, close.

Ben has used the Internet and phone to find a place on Mayne Island, just up a large hill from where I was last year. It has a narrow V-shaped panoramic view of Active Pass, and also looks over the north end of Galiano Island out across the Strait of Georgia to the mountains north of Vancouver. The view is a different version of the one I had last year, this time from further back, giving a more detached big-picture scan of boats, islands, water, and sky. The BC ferries are not so close and dominant here, and I'm curious to see how I adapt to this difference, with nonchalant ease or with more characteristic nostalgic longing. The day-to-day experimentation continues, and I live in hope that soon we'll get a better breed of scientists.

Minutes after we settle in, we watch a young eagle, not yet white-headed or tailed, riding the wind over the clearing in front of us, back and forth, up and down. Some paths have better signposts than others.

✳   ✳   ✳

On this visit, I read more of the island's history and interact more with people, in grocery stores and restaurants, in the bakery and artists' stands, and in the bookstore. The shell has not been pulled over my head this time, and as is in the nature of shells and those who use them, I miss it.

One of the interactive stops is at a new bookstore that Ben finds on our first day, a small room at the front of Springwater Lodge selling used and new books that have been picked with care. One of the things I like to do, am compelled to do, is to have a few books lined up in whatever room is providing shelter that day. On this Easter and Passover weekend, and without the slightest knowledge of the owner, I become a partner in this bookstore filled with fine writers all backdropped by a view of Miners Bay wharf and the narrow twisting boat-filled Active Pass. I buy four books, and am pleased when my new business partner glances at my face and says, "Great choices!" Two are by Susan Sontag, *I, Etcetera* and *Under the Sign of Saturn*, *A Short Walk in the Hindu Kush* by Eric Newby, and *To Timbuktu* by Mark Jenkins. These, along with John Ralston Saul's *Voltaire's Bastards*, and two guidebooks, *The Southern Gulf Islands of British Columbia* and *Where to Eat in Canada*, get lined up at the end of the room next to the radio, between the door to the deck and the small side window. They give the room a stimulating academic attitude, one which I've always hoped to achieve, even if only for a short time, for example, just before lightning strikes. If I lived here, a bookcase would be an immediate purchase.

✳ ✳ ✳

This is my third visit to Mayne, and it seems that some things that were blurry are beginning to become clearer, more focused, partly due to my finally making the effort to read and listen, and partly (I suspect) due to time's gradual turning of the focus knob. I read that Mayne is the smallest of these southern Gulf Islands, and has about 850 people in the "off-season," and over 4,000 during the more popular summer months.

While the Johnny-and-Juan-come-latelys of England and Spain started parking their boats here just over two hundred years ago, aboriginal peoples have been around for at least five thousand years, probably more. We see on the map, and read, that the nearby

Tsartlip Band, on Helen Point, allows hikers to walk the wooded path next to the shore, if permission is asked and given. However, when we ask we are now told that the walk has been closed to visitors "so logging can go on." If we get it straight, there are no permanent residents on Band land, and we don't see a single aboriginal person on the island.

The guidebooks cast even more dark light on the nature of transience and expropriation. Miners Bay got its name from miners stopping to camp on the way to the Fraser River gold rush in the mid-1800s, with (it is implied) a few staying on as the rest followed their get-rich-quick vision. Many of the island's farms were owned by Japanese-Canadians in the 1930s, before they were taken to inland camps and their land was stolen by our resolutely racist Canadian government (i.e., by us) during World War II. If I ever get smart and lucky enough to achieve one of my many unrealized aims, namely to be a truly top-drawer thief, a genuine Fagin, then I must have a government doing the stealing for me, as they are so damn *good* at it, and (it would appear) beyond guilt or retribution.

There do not appear to be many Japanese faces on Mayne Island, at a glance, as their ghosts line up beside First Nations people and miners and Spanish ships, and the trees come tumbling down. It's definitely time for a dark beer or three, at the Springwater Lodge.

\* \* \*

When I was a kid in Nova Scotia, if anybody spoke of "the Island" it meant only one place, Prince Edward Island, PEI, *The Island*. Things become both more and less complicated if you spend your post-kid years moving around, where there are many islands, in people's mind's eyes and in reality. (When you get there, there is no "the" there and thank you, Gertrude Stein.)

In spite of knowing this, I still measure every island, literally and figuratively, against PEI. When I assess the geography, attitudes of communication and scenic views over the land and water, it is PEI that Mayne Island has to contend with, *not* the come-from-nearby pretenders of Galiano and Pender, and definitely not the semi-urban bliss of Salt Spring. (I did not include Saturna in this smack-up-side-the-head dismissal; it is difficult to get to, has few amenities of any kind, and its population is right up against zip. I like Saturna.) Mayne comes out of this comparison looking ok, and I even put it on the scale with the *real* PEI, and not the noxious Anne and capitalistic Cavendish segments. Even then, even when measured against Montague, North Rustico, St. Peter's Bay, and Tyne Valley, Mayne Island can *still* hold its own. This is high praise.

One of the recurrent inner debates, as I angle back towards an ocean in search of rotting seaweed to nestle in amongst, is about the liberal/conservative and pseudo/genuine poles of my own personal wheel of meaning. (In case there's any confusion, let me offer easy help: liberal is good and conservative is bad, *but* pseudo is bad and genuine is good. Can you see the blister-causing rub about to kick in? PEI is conservative *and* genuine, an awkward yet familiar combination, as is the reverse. While Mayne is . . . ? *That's* what I'm trying to find out.)

For example, the Health Centre on Mayne has a physician who works from 8 a.m. to 1 p.m., four days a week. There is a "first-call nurse," whose hours and duties are not given. Laboratory services are from 7:30 to 10:30 a.m. on Mondays only. "By appointment only" one can also get to see an assortment of other health care practitioners, including, (alphabetically listed in the local paper's ad), an Acupuncturist one day a week, an Alcohol and Drug Counselor one day a week, a Chiropractor one day a month, a Family Counselor one day a week, a Massage Therapist two days a week, a Public Health Nurse two days a month, and a Physiotherapist four days a week. (The only way I can figure that the Public Health Nurse leapt ahead of the Physiotherapist, alphabetically speaking, is if we go for PHN and PT; otherwise, it must be some personal humility and/or power-based interaction in progress.) What is one to make of all this, in a country where many communities with difficult access and huge burdens of preventable illness might have two or three of these, if they are sort-of-lucky? I line up my wheel of meaning, the liberal-pseudo-conservative-genuine one, and give it one almighty spinning tug.

In a book on *Hiking the Gulf Islands* by Charles Kahn, the following paragraph stands out and rings true:

> "Most of Mayne is privately owned. It has no provincial parks, no ecological reserves, and little Crown land. A new regional park offers some hiking potential for residents and visitors, but the few local parks are very small. It is a shame that more of Mayne has not been preserved for public use."

Perhaps, just perhaps, I need a few more categories on my wheel of meaning, including the shame/grace continuum. I glance over my shoulder to see if the wheel is still spinning, and it is. I'm not surprised to see that it appears to have speeded up.

✳ ✳ ✳

Near the end of our visit, Ben and I find the path to Edith Point, but not without having to ask for directions. The hiking guidebook says:

> "The peninsula leading to Edith Point is private land, but you are free to explore the foreshore. The access to this beach is a narrow, tunnel-like path through the trees, rather than a road. Watch carefully for it on Campbell Bay Road; it's easy to miss."

It's also worth finding, with rocky ledges giving a view east out over the Canada-United States International Boundary, characterized on the maps as a thick dotted line on the water. We try in vain to spot the watery dots. We do see a seal swimming near the shore, head-up and then gone under, then head-up, cruising the shore. We have a picnic lunch, read books, take photos, debate the judgmental aspects of various wheels-of-meaning, and get ourselves scrutinized by an otter.

The otter has swum by, very close to shore and stopping in the water to look directly at us. Our cross-species telepathic translators are fully charged and well maintained, so we can clearly hear Buddy's thoughts: "What *is* it with you people? Do you not know what 'private land' means? Is the concept of 'foreshore' completely beyond you? God, the ferries from the mainland all should be burned." We stay deadpan, so she/he doesn't know we can hear every word.

This otter is a good-natured landlord, though, and we don't get evicted. We *do* get scrutinized. It climbs out on the rocks to look us over, wanders back and forth on the terraced ledges behind us, and not too far behind, either. After about fifteen minutes of this, we hear the thought, "Oh, what the hell, let them be, harmless peasants!" The otter goes back to the water, to swim around the point into Campbell Bay.

We let out a peasant-like collective sigh of close-call relief. I vow to look up "foreshore" when I get home to the land-locked Lake of the Woods, as I have not got the faintest clue what it is. I also make a note to buy Ben a copy of *Ring of Bright Water*, which tells of other landlord otters.

✳   ✳   ✳

About a year later, a friend who is wise and aware of eagles came to visit at my place in Kenora. I showed him the eagle feather from the top of the steep hill on Mayne Island and told of the encounters. He asked questions about how the place and the time in my life made me feel, about changes and continuities, about my wheel of meanings and how it might intersect with the eagle's. The only conclusion we reached was that it was an important event for me, this eagle's visit, and I was pleased to leave it at that. I offered my friend the feather, but he left it with me, for now.

I added another continuum to my spinning wheel, importance and loss, and sensed the wheel move along, as it must.

*Miners Bay, British Columbia*
*Mayne Island, British Columbia*

# *Mobility*

*"Where my guides lead me in kindness*
*I follow, follow lightly,*
*and there are no footprints*
*in the dust behind us."*
                    *— Ursula K. Le Guin,*
                        *in The Telling*

*"When there's no comin'*
*And there's no goin' . . .*
*And when heart is open*
*You will change . . . "*
                    *— Van Morrison,*
                        *in Common One*

# Truly Flabby Nocturnes for the Road

*M*y father spent twenty years of his adult life as a travelling salesman, as the nonchalantly sexist vocabulary of the 1940s and 1950s labelled that occupation. His business card used a different term, stating that he was a manufacturer's representative. The Maritimes was his territory, and home hardware was his line, so I grew up hearing bits of news about Moncton and Charlottetown, Yarmouth, Sydney, Truro, Saint John, Summerside, and Antigonish, mixed in with how well the pots and hammers were moving, at his 5% commission plus no salary. When he would tell of his trips, which had him on the road over half the time of his and our shared life, the hotels and restaurants and especially the highway would sound exciting and full of meaning.

I craved the meaning, any old meaning at all would do, and so coaxed him to tell me, again, of a particularly adroit parallel-parking maneuver, in which our twelve-foot car was shoe-horned into a twelve-foot-and-one-inch space, with no touch of any other vehicle, as if Disney had just elevated the car and oh so gently placed it down in the barely adequate space.

In the days before cruise control, my father could keep the speedometer needle unwavering on sixty mph, not a flicker as we went up and down Maritime hills, around bends back and forth, enough to make a slalom skier proud. I've seen him do it.

To be fair to my father, (itself a touchy and difficult maneuver), he never did pretend that the road was not a lonely and frequently boring place to live. I think he was addicted to the mobility, however, and to the possibility of essential meaning randomly found, but I didn't get the chance to ask him because he died at the time I was beginning to explore the possibility of paradox and of repetitive mobile traps, and the linked fact that things may indeed be as they appear if only you can learn to see them.

For the last thirty-five years I've been on the road, in travelling sales, using ineffectual neo-Western biomedical concepts as the loss leader. The lines I distribute include Public Health as social justice, image gathering as a means of achieving clarity, vulnerability as a necessity in meaningful human communication, and a foundational primary-line conviction that unless curiosity and compassion are balanced in an individual and in a species, the results are monstrous. Some lines are moving better than others.

My territory has included the Maritimes, Labrador and Newfoundland (as it *should* be called – and the first shall come first), parts of the Arctic, Manitoba and northwestern Ontario, and the highways between Toronto and Vancouver. I am addicted to the road, and I occasionally wonder if my father would shake his head ruefully or be pleased, or both. I wish I knew, and again and again vow to make sure my daughters know, all they are willing to hear.

The Canadian road is a convoluted one, and I'm on it about half of my time. In the past few months, the stops (and starts) have included Sechelt, Vancouver, Whitehorse, Banff, Dawson Creek, Yellowknife, Calgary, Saskatoon, Winnipeg, much of northwestern Ontario, Toronto, Montreal, Saint John, Grand Manan, Charlottetown, Truro and environs, and Middle Musquodobit. There are few better sights than a view of the highway unfolding or the lit-up, straight-arrow, "come-on-*in*" beckoning of an airport runway as the final approach is made. Don't addicts *always* feel that way?

A friend asked if I too don't get lonely and bored, as my father surely did, and I said yes, of course I do, even embellishing the acknowledgement with my description of a balding and bearded squirrel on a treadmill, duped into obligatory movement and illusionary purpose. However, I do prize my independence and the kaleidoscopic nature of my days, as I suspect my father did. Loneliness, too, is relative, and the fact that I'm on a bilateral first-name basis with the porter in Medicine Hat, the cashier at the Market Garden cafeteria in Toronto (who recently asked, again, how my "beautiful daughters" are doing), the server in Banff's dining room, and the desk clerk in Vancouver does take the edge away from the lonely-soldier-of-the-highway persona.

The challenge that *does* sting, however, due to its damning nature, is that I may be in hiding on the road, in retreat from stable and lasting commitments to people and places, and to self. When "friends" bring this up I think on it, even if they are destructive and self-serving at the time. When these analytic others start feeling overly smug about the accuracy of their analysis, I query the commitment and excitement of *their* time. Our conversations often end at about this point, but not always. The few rare ones who are willing to battle doubt and continue caring, and will allow me to do so, are those who understand the road and how to share it, even from a distance.

Leaving Portage la Prairie a while ago, at that post-sunset pre-dark time of day, (the season is of no recollection or relevance to me, so you colour it in, it's yours to make relevant or to abandon), there was a long freight train moving west, coming toward me as I drove east toward Kenora. It was about two kilometres south of the highway, with the three triangulated headlights brightly on, a slow-moving straight line of train on the incredibly flat prairie. As our directions passed, the train became a part of the horizon, in thickening blue light. On my tape player I had George Shearing's version of

Erik Satie's "Gymnopedies," leading to a precisely improvised jazz quartet of piano and train and light and prairie.

When I got home, I felt that it would be useful to do some research on Erik Satie, rather than leaving all the work to George Shearing. I read that Satie was born in Hanfleur, France, in 1866, and that eventually he rejected the formality and snobbery of the music of the 1800s. He thumbed his nose at the "experts" of the day by giving such titles to his pieces as "Truly Flabby Preludes for a Dog," and detailing tongue-in-both-cheeks performance instructions, such as "to be played like a nightingale with a toothache." I wish he had seen the prairie, as part of the quartet playing in gathering-dusk tones.

A colleague, who moved several steps west over twenty years ago, once shared a small plane with me, flying from St. Therese Point to Winnipeg. We agreed, quickly and completely, that we both loved the space and reach of the high wide sky, and the counterpoint angular boreal forest and rock-juts strategically placed latitudinally above the prairie. Although I still, and will always, belong to the Maritimes and Labrador, I also agree with our shared immigrants' conversion, and also with Erik Satie's blind description of a straight-line relaxed down-home train as it labours off into blue dark. Images like that only come from the road, and it's good to be here.

*highway-edge motel, Saskatchewan*

# *Who They Are*

---

*I*'d been stuck for the night at Prawda, Manitoba, on my way back home from Winnipeg to Kenora, as the highway had been closed in a snowstorm. I should have listened to Ben, police broadcasts, weather reports, and Highway Department advisories, all of which said, "Stay put in Winnipeg, you idiot." I didn't listen.

As I attempted to start out for Kenora from the Prawda motel in the morning, with the storm over but the roads still deep in snow, it was so cold that one of my vehicle's front wheels wouldn't turn. It was frozen, and I had to go back and forth, a few inches at a time, to coax it free. The highway was still "closed," but the truckers at the Prawda coffee shop told me that the OPP and the RCMP are so understaffed that they don't barricade the road or enforce the closure. They just announce it, proclaim it, and then we're on our own. I got the heater cranked up, aimed all unfrozen wheels true east and left, on my own.

The driving was not that bad, with one lane open and scattered mid-road drifts and a wonderful absence of traffic, possibly due to the road closure. I had extra clothes tucked into the back seat and the trunk, along with a blanket and candles and a bit of food, and an unopened thick novel, so even if I got stuck or broke down I was laughing, or at least chortling ruefully.

The ride to Kenora was a clear breeze but ever so cold. As I approached the town, a tall man was walking on the edge of the narrow single open lane, and he turned to look at me as I eased by. I stopped to ask if he wanted a ride, and he got in, saying nothing. He was wearing a fur cap with the earflaps down, a warm looking old parka, and good heavy once-white snow-boots. He had a series of little icicles hanging from his beard and moustache, all around his nose and mouth, and he was shivering.

I turned the heat up by several notches. The man wasn't talking, and neither was I. There was now a heavy wood-smoke odour in the car, a smell I know and respect. "You have a wood stove," I said, not asking a question. He started to talk, looking straight ahead at the one open lane of road, and told me of his tent in the woods, just a couple of miles back from where I picked him up. He'd been there since summer and found it to be safe and warm. "They can't find me there," he said, and I didn't ask who they are. I know who they are.

"Where do you work?" he asked. I told him, and then sensing that the words meant nothing, I added, "Just in behind the hospital. Do you want a ride into town, or is the hospital road ok?"

"You a doctor?" he asked. When I said, "yes," he asked if I'm a psychiatrist.

"No, I'm not."

"You know Dr. McDonald at Toronto Psychiatric? He's a good person."

We sat for a couple of minutes at the turnoff, as he told me of Dr. McDonald's good points. Then he got out, held the door open and looked at me for the first time, nodded, closed the door, and walked toward town.

*Kenora, Ontario*

150

# *Necessary Purpose*

*T*he Sunset Inn in Sioux Lookout, Ontario, has a wing of non-smoking rooms on the second floor, and one side of this wing looks west out over Pelican Lake, from the south end of town. In the summer you can watch many single-engine Otters and Cessnas and occasional Beavers and Turbo-Beavers as they fill with people and then empty, angle in and out from the dock, and take off and land on the lake. You can watch this wide-sweeping purposeful dance from a room window or from a bench at the water's edge by the Tourist Bureau across the street from the hotel. In the winter the lake becomes a highway for snowmobiles, roaring, speeding for the fun of it, an auditory nuisance but I can't bring myself to hate them, having been fully introduced to their *real* purpose in Labrador. There the machines are used to go from place to place, as there are scarce options, and to help in the gathering of wood, water and food. They are necessary in Labrador, Nunavut, the NWT, and parts of elsewhere, and that allows me a thin skim of affection.

This nagging problem of necessity of purpose flicks in and out of view in room #241 of the Sunset Inn on a cold winter evening. I have not managed to push myself into going for a walk, not even the usual one out through town and back across the lake, nor have I gone to push weights at the sports centre in the arena. It looks like I'm not even going to be able to get it together enough to go for supper at the Forest Inn or the Chinese-food place downtown. It would appear that I've got the hotel-room blues, the **what**-*am-I-doing-here* doldrums. I verify this diagnosis by eating a bag of chips with a Coke, the standard diet for a public-health type bent on going over to the dark side. To confirm this, I do repetitive and unnecessary paperwork and watch television situation-inanities. All I need is a flat of cigarettes with no filters and a six-pack of warm beer, along with some deliciously unsafe sex, to complete the full-throttle-into-hell's-own-flames picture.

My kids, Jan from Calgary and Sarah from Toronto, come to the rescue via the phone. As often as I've cursed Alex Bell over the decades for the invention of this intrusive blight on the psychic landscape, I have to grudgingly admit that the telephone can occasionally be of use, rarely but really. This is one of those times.

Sarah calls first, getting my whereabouts from my home answering machine, to tell me of a soup she's just made, thick with vegetables and purposeful in its low-calorie intensity. It will last all week. She's pleased with herself, and with me as I gave her the pot and the recipe, one neo-cook to another. We have a friendly and funny exchange about soup and other sustenance realities. This is a person who will insist on having a major influence on the course of her own life, from dance to dinner, and I'm happy to know her and to be on the receiving end of her call, anytime.

Jan phones to room #241 about an hour later, and I resist asking if Sarah has sent out a Pete-alert as it doesn't matter and I don't need to know even if she did, unless they need to tell me. We spontaneously get into a serious discussion of my generation's workforce choices versus hers. We conclude, and not for the first or last time, that my whole gang of boomers had and continue to have many more job opportunities but at the cost of our narrowness, a stunted, low-risk, anti-creative "security" that undermines personal growth

152

and depth but *does* pay the bills, circling back to that particular necessary purpose. Her crowd, however, have little long-term security as they learn to be versatile enough to dance in many productions, so to speak. I prefer her wealth of options, which as Jan quickly points out with good-humoured accuracy is easy for me to say. "From the elite and secure comfort of room 241," I counter, and we chuckle together. We know what we mean.

I feel much better and send a mental I.O.U. to my daughters. Before going to sleep, having decided to-hell-with-supper, I read from the two books I've brought along, Katy Payne's *Silent Thunder*, a moving personal account of her work with African elephants, and Roger Payne's *Among Whales*, about his studies of whales in several oceans, especially off the coast of South America. These two people were married to each other for a long time and now are not. I enjoy going back and forth from book to book, looking for clues to the shades of that relationship. I'm specifically looking for and hoping for signs of mutual respect and gratitude and (dare I hope?) affection. (There *are* risks to putting oneself into the mix of other people's work. I look in vain.) This is almost as much painful fun as their portrayals of the fragile complexities of whale and elephant social lives and methods of communication, with the animals' extreme vulnerability to murderous, stupid, and uncaring humans. Both authors keep the clues to the origins, course and demise of their relationship well buried, and I send a mute voyeur's complaint in their direction. It is an evening of gratitudes, debts, and mute complaints.

Tomorrow, I'm going to exercise and eat healthy and stay clear of the undertow of boomer angst. I might even get into work on time. We'll see about all of these, in the morning.

*Sioux Lookout, Ontario*

153

# *Doom is Imminent*

*T*he workshop in Sioux Lookout on "mold in residential set-
tings" (I'm not making it up) finishes at about 5 p.m., just as
it's getting dark and the snow is thickening. I'm tempted to
stay overnight, to do the smart thing and call ahead pleading
"weather," thereby skipping the meetings scheduled for tomorrow
with family docs in Fort Frances and Emo and Rainy River. The
temptation to do the smart thing is once again easily resisted and I
buckle up, get the radio locked on CBC, and aim for downtown
Rainy River, over four hundred kilometres away.

At 10:15 p.m. I pull into Rainy River stiff from the car and the
twisting slippery road, and hungry, ready to eat some of the food I
bought at the grocery store in Dryden. I'm also tired enough to not
even bother trying to sort out and categorize the mélange of images
from five hours of CBC radio's *News, As It Happens, This Morning
Tonight*, and *Ideas*. I'm swamped with competing angles of view and
have the need to shut it down, eat a sandwich, read a book, and then
sleep the night away, preferably all of it.

They've lost my reservation at the motel, or we "never made one." Who can sort out these eternal questions? Not me, that's for damn sure, and I resign myself to permanent ignorance regarding lost virtue, silent friends, and unrecorded or unmade reservations as I go back out into the blowing snow and -25°C chill. There's nowhere else in town to stay so I point the car at the Canada/USA border, just a few kilometres away.

Baudette, Minnesota, is on the American side of the river-border, the flowing in summer and frozen in winter Rainy River, and I ease over the bridge and up to the American border guard with Joni Mitchell's plea for a "river to skate away on" playing background in my inner soundtrack. It's 11 p.m. The border guard gives me an eyebrow-raised silent question, and I tell him I *really* need a bed and where I'm from and why, and how long I'll be staying in the States and why, possibly looking the whole time like I'm about to cry.

"We're not allowed to recommend any particular place to stay," he says, as he prepares to wave me into his country. I haven't asked about places to stay because I haven't thought that far ahead.

"So," he says, "I'm definitely *not* recommending that you drive to the first stop sign, turn right, go straight for about three miles, and stay at the big new place on your left." I smile at him, finally seeing a person and not just an obstacle, adding, "It's reassuring to see that the borders are being guarded by people who give our rules the respect they deserve. Thanks. I appreciate it."

"Goodnight," he says, unsmiling through everything. "Get some rest."

At the AmericInn all the regular rooms are full. The desk clerk does a quick size-up and offers me the Lake of the Woods Suite, at a bit more than half price. (I cultivate the doom-is-imminent look. It only fails me with bankers and small-town municipal politicians, those two being the epitome of right-wing, self-serving, heartless scoundrels, but I may be slandering the bankers). The suite has a huge bedroom with a large window looking over snowy Minnesota fields and a kitchen/living room area with bathroom and TV attached. I'm home.

As I eat my sandwiches, fruit and yogurt at midnight, I open the mail I picked up at 8 p.m. the prior evening in Kenora as I was leaving for Sioux Lookout, and then stuffed in my briefcase, since forgotten. In the midst of the bills and appeals for funds and magazines is a letter from a friend I haven't seen in over seven years. There are no accidental connections, and this letter connects to one of the radio rivers that I skated away on a few hours ago, regarding the nature of lasting friendship. The letter from my friend tells of real events in her life and then asks, in a matter-of-fact fashion, which is obviously not a put-down, how I'm doing with "your sadness." I turn off the TV in Suite 201 of the AmericInn in Baudette and remember the last time we saw each other. She's right. I was sad.

It was in the lobby of a performance place in St. John's, Newfoundland, and I'd come to watch some members of the group Figgy Duff sing their harmonious and bitter songs. I had mostly come, though, to simply share time with someone I cared for. During the intermission it finally became fully evident to me that things were completely wrong, and not just the result of debatable and fixable issues as I'd been pretending. This person did not want to be seen with me, for several reasons. Some of these reasons I could see to be all too true, while others were not true, at least not for me. She was ashamed of me, and I felt betrayed and equally ashamed of her. We were empty, finished.

In the midst of this standing in a lonely lobby while dashed-on-the-rocks-of-reality diagnostic scan, I looked up to see another friend, a person I hadn't seen in several years, the writer of the letter now opened in Baudette. She spotted me at the same time and gave a spontaneous hug and direct-eye smile in midst of the crowded lobby, in the midst of people she knew and more she didn't. The contrast was striking and educational. I felt rescued and must have shown it on my face, as both concern and kindness were in evidence on *her* face, as we stood together for about three minutes in total. I haven't seen her since and am looking forward to answering this letter, to tell her I'm not so sad anymore, and perhaps I'll even be able to share a figurative smile and hug and eye contact, from afar.

Earlier in the evening, as I was listening to the CBC *Ideas* discussion of friendship and betrayal, on the road near the winter-closed lakeside resorts on the outskirts of Nestor Falls, I tried to figure out just what made a "true friend" true, anyway. I've betrayed people I called friends and am regretful and diminished but am also not sure *why* I went wrong, why I choose those particular actions and attitudes. It is also useful to me to know that there are other friends I have not betrayed, people I have kept faith with despite hurt, and silence, and time. I don't know why the categories of betrayed and not betrayed exist, except for accident and whim. It seems likely that the ones who haven't been true to me also weren't sure of the reasons behind what they were doing, or not doing. I'm in search of an epigram. I'll have to wait for the appropriate *Ideas* program on CBC to give me the lead line on that one, maybe, later.

*Baudette, Minnesota*
*Rainy River, Ontario*

# *Echoes*

*I*t's a Sunday in late March, and I'm on the road.

Last night, having left Calgary by car aiming east at 11 p.m., I'd been tempted to drive right through to Kenora, with a full moon to illuminate the suicidal deer and only eighteen hours to go, or some such illusionary nonstop number. Alberta's wealth and accompanying heightened sense of social responsibility has led to a wonderful-wide divided highway so it should have been an opening-gambit breeze, but it wasn't. I ran out of wakefulness at Brooks, only an hour's drive west of Medicine Hat. The midnight-shift desk clerk at the shiny new Holiday Inn Express said I looked tired, at 2 a.m., and gave me a huge room at a good price.

The next morning, this morning, I'm up and showered and gone in twenty minutes, walking across the blowing parking lot at 8 a.m., keeping time to the wafting fragrance of manure and the threat of freezing rain. No problem, none of it, as I've got two coffees to hand, a cooler on the passenger seat full of adequate snacks, and CBC radio on the dial. There's a long highway day ahead of me, over 1,400 kilometres, and I'm excited at the prospect of an entire day of listening to the CBC. The thoughtful images are sure to come thick and fast, or even thick and slow but definitely not too skinny, and my greatest risk is one of conceptual overload.

The Regina station, 540 on AM, is incredibly strong, either that or the radio-god harmonics line up just right for me, over and over, because from Brandon to Calgary I can get 540, summer or winter. The only time I abandon it is when the Blue Jays are playing, and surely *that* can't count as fickle or unfaithful – it's baseball, after all. On this blowing wet-snow and manure-odour early morning I arrange coffee and seat belt, snack access and CBC dial, and off I go, accompanied.

For the next fifteen hours, all the way to Kenora, I listen to CBC One, rarely turning it off except for occasional self-indulgent bursts of silence, or Van Morrison's "Washing Windows" song on tape, several times in a row. I hear *This Morning*, with Michael Enright's ironic disdain competing with the Mother Corp's earnestness, and *Tapestry* then making it all too clear who won *that* competition. CBC *News* plays over and over, and episodic weather (but I can see it and my own wheels can feel it, so I know better), Robin Brown's thoughtful sports-show *The Inside Track*, Rex Murphy doing his polyglot improvisational vocal-jazz-turn on *Cross-Country Check-Up*, (this is the show that most often leads to necessary episodes of give-me-a-break turn-off-the-radio silence, as two hours of non-stop-Rex is like a full meal of sourdough cheesecake), Rick Phillips' wildly opinionated and completely excellent classical music *Sound Advice*, and Eric Friesen's *Concert Hall*, which on this day features six miniature funeral and/or impending-death pieces by Bach. Throughout the day, there are more reverberations, predictions, echoes, bullshit, and wise words blindly aimed my way than I'm capable of hearing, and I'm thankful for this, all of it.

The echoes come in various forms. Between Swift Current and Regina a woman is walking a bike, angling it across a snow-sprinkled brown-grass field, probably moving from one road to another. She is wearing a yellow and black jacket and is quite close to the road I'm on; my highway is the edge of her field, as we pass each other. As I go by at 110 km/hr I can see her face clearly and without doubt, she is smiling. She's alone and she's smiling, as her own echoes play for her own benefit. She doesn't appear to notice me, our eyes do not meet, and I'm guessing that she is unaware of the gray car angling fast toward and then away from her route.

Something about her jacket and her walk and especially her smile reminds me of a missing friend in Labrador. As soon as the highway and CBC will allow it, maybe from a meal stop in Regina, I'm going to call and write Janet in L'Anse au Clair. We take and make our connections as we find them, as best we can.

*Regina, Saskatchewan*

# *Lac des Mille Lacs*

*J*.P. Cormier plays fiddle and guitar at the Winnipeg Folk Festival, and it's a treat to listen and watch. He's a wizard at making the strings vibrate, but that's only part of it. The other part is that he's from Cape Breton. He's from close to home, where I'm from. I follow him around the small outdoor stages he plays over the four-day July festival, watching the interactions he has with the music and instruments, and also watching how he copes with praise, with other shining stars on the stage at the same time in the "workshops," with hot days and rain delays, and with being accompanied by his partner/spouse on keyboard. He copes very well.

J.P. is a large man, side-burned and gruff, with a stereotypic biker appearance even if he never once gripped a handlebar. He has Cape Breton in his voice as he talks of his drinking days and of living for years in the U.S.A. He gives the impression of rueful delight at having rejected both of these pasts. The memories aren't so bad and the present can only get better, a Cape Breton creed. He scatters routine Nova Scotian curses throughout his between-time chats, and he'd probably be startled if anyone took offense at such ordinary language, but even then I doubt if he'd change one jeestly word. At any rate, there are probably more people here from worldly Minnesota than from all of Carmen, Winkler, Morden, and Steinbach combined, so what the hell, let 'er rip, J.P.

He does, he tears it up good on several stages and through different styles and attitudes and instruments and shared workshop topics. I feel like I'm back home as I watch, and it would be good to be able to thank him so, as the next best thing, I buy a couple of his CDs.

\*   \*   \*

A couple of months later I'm driving back to Kenora from a meeting in Thunder Bay, trying to get home before dark, before the moose hit the highway. I've skipped lunch and get hungry so I pull in for soup and a sandwich at Lac des Mille Lacs, a roadside stop on the long run between Thunder Bay and Ignace. As I'm hurrying through the snack a man and a woman come in, looking weary, more fed-up than hungry, and they aren't saying much to each other. I empathize with the trembling alienation of the long-distance driver so I suspend all judgments, and even as I recognize J.P. and his partner I shift my seat a bit so that I'm not looking over at their table, not eye-dropping on them. In my warped worldview this is an even bigger compliment than buying two CDs. It's a bended-knee, eyes-averted, neck-exposed tribute to a superior being, a rare tribute. I *do* hate that hero-worship crap, I truly do, but after a suppressed sigh of self-loathing I give in to it and let them eat away, unobserved.

As I go up to pay my bill so does J.P., and I haven't even timed it, I swear. He nods to me to go first, go ahead, and I nod back and do go first, us Nova Scotian boys being both taciturn *and* polite. After paying I turn to him and say, "I saw you play at the Winnipeg Festival, on a few stages, and I listen to your CDs. Your music is great; thanks for doing it." He looks startled, almost shocked, and I get a whipping-by image of Superman having some white-bearded-old-guy say to him, "Know what, Super? I saw you change from caper to Clark in that booth over there, and I think you are *real* fast." J.P. thanks me, shyly, seeming to be trying to find a spark of verbal energy, an escape from being road-whipped.

He tells me, briefly, of how many places they've played since then and how many times they've driven back and forth from Nova Scotia. I tell him that even though this particular 250-kilometre patch of highway seems endless, we all do appreciate having the chance to hear him play, and I thank him again. We shake hands and do a couple more nods, and I leave but not before I wish him huge good luck. He seems to know it's meant.

\*   \*   \*

Two years later I'm in Fort Frances, Ontario, just across the river from International Falls, Minnesota. I'm working. This involves eating crow, on this occasion several times in one day. "One crow sorrow, two crows joy," my mother used to chant, "three crows a wedding, four crows a boy." I'm also working the phones and listening to various grievances as they percolate up and down the hierarchical flights of fancy. I am not having fun.

On CBC radio from Thunder Bay in the early morning, it is mentioned that J.P. Cormier is playing in Fort Frances tonight. I don't get alert quickly enough to hear the where or when or the ticket outlets, none of that essential data, but I'm still feeling rescued. The second crow is circling.

Later I ask people for details, but no one knows, not the friendly Post Office person who directs my package of photos and other symbolic hugs to daughter Sarah and then even asks other people in the patient lineup behind me, not the La Place Rendez-Vous Hotel owner and staff who bring me lunch and who reassure me that there *is* some positive press coverage circulating to balance the negative, and definitely not the several others in the audible universe who are so intent on emphasizing my many flaws. I can't find out a thing, and work keeps getting in the way of this investigation. Then, Cindy overhears as I ask unsuspecting workers and clients for directions to J.P., and she takes pity. Cindy is not thrilled with the shape of her workday or with me, but she is a kind one, and kindness wins every time over pissed-off on the one-two-three-four sequence, a crow-based mantra.

Cindy has a season ticket, two of them in fact, and she is not going so she offers them to me. I'm told that the concert is sold out, and I now have two tickets; events are strange and various. Take a date Cindy advises, but I decline the advice and the second ticket, fearing communication more than solitude, a recurring theme.

I arrive at the high school auditorium at 7:28 for a 7:30 p.m. show, having misjudged a few directions. The place is packed so I immediately go to the very front, knowing that as true Canadians the residents of Fort Frances will have left the showy front seats with lots of space, especially for singletons. (I'm gambling that the front-row American International Falls crowd is staying home tonight.) I get the third row, stage level, aisle seat, with no one in front of me. I may be late, nonchalantly showy, alienated from my work, homesick for the Maritimes, and above-all a solo crow, but by damn I've got a great seat.

J.P. is looking relaxed and large, dressed in a red shirt with a black vest, charcoal jeans, and terrible red cowboy boots, which he claims to have stolen from Ashley MacIsaac, "and he's too small to get them back." These boots have silver jangly hanging parts on the heel. I hope they're stolen, especially from Ashley, but he still paid too much for them. "His hair is lighter than on the cover pictures," a woman behind me says to her daughter.

J.P.'s band is Hilda Chaisson Cormier. She is on the keyboard, making it hum and soar, a virtuoso accompanist, playful and challenging and interjecting, musically and verbally. They seem relaxed with each other, caring, neither one holding back. Hilda is leaving the flamboyance to J.P., looking classy in her long dark-blue jacket with the black trim, black pants and black shoes, not a flicker of stolen-red in sight. The pants are sparkly but only in an elegant and subtle on-stage manner. With her gentle teasing of husband J.P., her keyboard skill and her tiny size, combined with her striking attractiveness and quick bursts of illuminating grins, as well as one flurry of step dancing, Hilda has the crowd eating out of her hand, as does J.P.

J.P. sings and plays the guitar, fiddle, mandolin, and banjo, and while I admire and enjoy all he does, it's the guitar playing that makes me lean forward and gape. The guitar is a large square blond thing, and I'm reminded for an instant of people looking like their dogs. It was made in Newfoundland by the Garrison brothers, and J.P. praises them, saying they have allowed him to play this way. "It's hard to find something good to take on the road with you," he says, looking down at the guitar, and Hilda reacts in mock extravagant horror, mouth open, arms spread apart, pushing back her keyboard chair to walk away from the road forever, as the crowd laughs and applauds. "Sometimes, it doesn't pay to open your damn mouth at all," says J.P., deadpan. They have never been in Fort Frances before, but they have been at this spot on the road before, and they're having fun. So are we.

This is the start of a six-week tour, we're told, going west to Calgary and on to Yellowknife, and they're driving. They don't mention other stops, but there will be a bunch of them. Jan and I drove to Yellowknife two years ago, and we made the long and intense road a connection. Hilda and J.P. have a long hike ahead of them, and they'll have to work at it. I have the feeling that they know all this.

Only one person in the audience is from Cape Breton (J.P. asks), just down the way a bit from their place. Most in the packed hall have never been to Cape Breton, (J.P. asks, and people respond with a show of hands). "It's an easy ride," he says. "We got here."

The crowd seems to be enjoying their music. "I try to write true things," J.P. says, and I search Hilda's face; she agrees, you can see it. Right or wrong, one crowd or two, on the road or at home, she is a part of this truth.

At the break I go to the lobby to buy some CDs, one for sister Sue, one for Cindy, and one for me. I don't have cash, and they don't take plastic. I go back to my seat.

Later, after the skillful, respectful and funny second set and encore, I wait for the crowd to ease out and then go again to the CD-selling table in the lobby. Sure enough, J.P. and Hilda come out to talk and sign CDs. I wait. When the timing is right, I come up to him and say, "I have a proposal. I have no cash with me, and I'd like to take six CDs, but you'll have to trust me to send you a cheque." He looks at me, waiting for more. He's a big man, maybe younger than I thought, with sideburns and a moustache and a full chin-beard, a good face, as faces go, strong. "I met you last year, at Lac des Mille Lacs," I say, "at the diner." He smiles now, maintaining the eye contact, and says, "I remember you. Lake of a Thousand Lakes; yes." I have no idea if he's remembering, thinking that maybe after all you *can* bullshit a bullshitter. "You want *six*?" he asks. Indeed, yes, I do. No problem, he says, and gives me his mailing address in Cape Breton. We shake hands and I leave, six CDs in hand, nodding a thank you to Hilda as I go, two crows, joy.

*Bird's Hill Park, Manitoba*
*Lac des Mille Lacs, Ontario*
*Fort Frances, Ontario*

# Did You Leave the Tip?

Jan and I are lined up at Subway on a hot Saturday afternoon in Kenora. This is the edible "subway," not the other one that goes under the railroad tracks near the high school. Only true long-time Kenora folk can hear some subtle vocal inflection differentiating the two, for instance when saying, "down by the subway."

"Which one?" I always ask, playing the role of dumb come-from-away for all its worth. (It's not worth a lot.)

This is a July holiday weekend and the town is thick with people, residents and tourists and Manitoban "summer people." The harbour is alive with people in small boats, some to or from shopping at Safeway, others going to the laundromat or Canadian Tire or the harbourfront shops and restaurants, while many are just out for a run, a cruise. There is a steady high-speed skim-by at the narrows between the Lakeside area and Coney Island, with a few politely and prudently slowing but most just whipping through; they've been here before, thank you.

Subway is booming, with a long line-up inside and more people thinking about it out on the sunny sidewalk. The staff appear to hate this popularity, as they obviously want to be out on the sidewalk, too. They share this sentiment freely by sighing often, loudly and with conviction, and by then asking, "What do you *want?*," emphasis full on the "want," as if we're panhandling.

Jan and I are part of a line of seven or eight people. There were a few ahead of us when we came in, but who-knows-who-is-where in the disorderly evolution of fast-food distribution? We supplicants are all strung-out along the counter, starting at the bread ovens and ending at the cash register. Directly in front of us is a little kid, aged six or seven, wearing a ball cap, not on backwards. His clothes all look too big for him – shirt, pants, sneakers – all in search of the kid's major growth spurt or a larger person.

Jan has already given her order and is up along paying for it, while I'm into my chant-like recitation of things wanted and not when I realize that the little kid is still standing there. His head is below the high counter-top so he's probably been missed, overlooked. He has coins in his hand and is just standing, waiting. I stop my order and say to him, "I'm sorry. Did I jump in ahead of you?" but he only glances at me, startled, shy, and then looks away without speaking, not sure what I mean. Even if he does know, he's maybe wondering why I'm giving up my rightful big-people entitlement. The place is noisy but I hear one staff say to another, "Did you get the kid?" The other staff says, "No, I thought he was with them," with a slight nod at me and Jan. Nobody cares much, least of all the kid. He just wants some food, and hold the fuss.

After getting his sandwich and pop, the kid goes to join a slightly older and bigger boy, and I'm guessing it's his brother judging by the way they barely speak but nevertheless seem to support each other. They sit at the window-counter to eat, and Jan and I do too. When they go, the kid leaves some coins, his change, but he's long-gone before I notice. Something tells me that this was not intended to be a tip. It was an accident.

I give the money to the least morose staff person, describing who left it. The staff and new line of customers look at me like I've lost my mind. I haven't, and I'm betting the kid's out $1.45.

*Kenora, Ontario*

# *Boundaries*

*T*he nude beach at Hanlan's Point on Toronto Island is not called a nude beach; it is called a clothing-optional beach. Most of us opt to do without, but a few tourists amble by with some of their parts encased in cloth, peering about or studying the tips of their toes as if they were at a corrupt zoo. They are ignored.

It's another hot, humid summer in Toronto, and in the month I live on the Island, I go to the optional beach most days, for an hour or three each time. The sandy area is surrounded by trees, lake and fence, with official posted signs indicating where clothes are needed and where there are options.

The demographics of the beach are interesting, for those of us dedicated to free theatre. Well over fifty percent of the people on the kilometre-long stretch of sand are gay males, travelling in groups or pairs or as singletons. Some of these men spend much of their time walking back and forth at the water's edge. On most days there are women on the beach, but they are a definite minority. They usually are in groups or with males, and about half of the women wear bathing-suit bottoms. Occasionally a woman is alone, and she radiates calm comfort in her solitude, or so I read it. On a few days, very few, adults bring young children, and they are easily naked and re-laxed. Every day, there are several older people and most of these are regulars, here every sunny day and usually going to the same part of the beach and talking with many of the same people, also relaxed in their complete and unvaried brown skin that apparently disdains wrinkles and skin cancer. A few people swim, as the water is warm and clear, ostensibly free of risk.

Over the month, it becomes apparent to me that Toronto is an urban society in search of opportunities to remove its clothing. For some, Hanlan's Point is a refuge, connected in spirit to Manitoba's Patricia Beach and Vancouver's Wreck Beach, and to others.

On one of my last days of staying on the Island and visiting the beach, I get to say separate goodbyes to three people – a man my age, a woman ten or fifteen years older than me, and a younger woman. The older woman tells me about her garden in the city, just across the water by ferry to that other world. She is wearing large gold-rimmed glasses and has a direct gaze and speech, and I can easily imagine her garden being well cared for. Last year, she was able to come here to the beach until late in October. Later, the younger woman comes over to where I'm sitting alone at a picnic ta-ble. We sit beside each other facing the water and the sun, talking about taboos and boundaries, privacy and intrusion, friendliness and flirtation, self-respect and self-loathing. We talk comfortably and then go in separate directions. We'll never see each other again.

The last person I speak with is a white-bearded, slim, fit man with a quick full smile. During my month on Toronto Island, he and I have progressed from nodding to speaking, on the beach and on other parts of the five-kilometre-long mid-harbour archipelago. He lives here, all the time, on Ward's Island, at the very other end. We talk and smile and listen. I say, "I hope to see you again, maybe next year." Then I get dressed and go home to pack.

*Toronto Island, Ontario*

# *Do We Not Flinch?*

*I*t's a moderately hot summer day in Winnipeg, with a slight breeze and clear sky, not humid, a classic. I'm on my lunch break and have just had a pasta and soup combination at De Luca's restaurant on Portage Ave. This is a wonderful place, noisy and crowded, in a second-floor loft at the back of a popular Italian-heritage grocery store. The food is served cafeteria style, and the lunch crowd shares a few large round tables, strangers and friends sitting together, seven or eight to a table, with their pasta, pizza, soup, baskets of crusty bread, and wine or water and caffe latte. Some talk and some eat in silence. The room adapts with ease, a warm and comfortable place.

After I leave all this, I'm feeling good about my world, standing in line at the bank on the corner of Arlington and Portage, tapped-out but not minding, not even a little bit. I'm in a long line and am casually watching, a reflex, noting people's stances and the attitudes they reveal, their ways of dealing with waiting and money and each other. The bank feels like an extension of De Luca's restaurant, a sustaining place of relaxed mutual support. (I don't always get this feeling in banks.)

The man directly in front of me is in his early-to-mid twenties, muscled, dressed in a t-shirt and shorts and sandals, and he's closed-off, his walls are up. Another man comes in from the street and he's peering around at the lines of people, looking for someone. He is tall, also muscled, dressed in jeans, t-shirt and sneakers. He spots the man in front of me and moves towards us. I step back, to let him in, to let him join someone I have quickly assumed to be his friend. The newcomer looks at me, seeing my movement, but he doesn't smile, doesn't nod or say thanks. Instead, he steps closer to me and says, "If you cut us, do we not bleed? If you shun us, do we not hurt?" By now he's face to face, and angry. He is brown-skinned, as is the man standing in front of me. I am white.

I pause, confused, until it clicks in and I recognize the conflicting assumptions. I step even closer to him, nose to nose, also angry and say, "You've made a mistake. I saw you recognize him and was stepping back to let you in, that's all. You should look more carefully before you flash the attitude. Now, do you want to get in line or do you want to go outside and talk about it some more?" He moves back, ready to "go outside," no sweat, but then seems to change his mind and just steps into the line in front of me. I'm betting that his decision has been rapid and casual, and has very little to do with me. He starts to talk to the other man, with much animation, about some place they're going, ignoring me with studied ease. He is not bleeding. I restrain the urge to correct his Shakespeare, deciding to not push my luck. After a glance at his biceps, it's an easy decision.

Leaving the bank, with money in my pocket but feeling considerably impoverished, the hot sun on the sidewalk and the general glare of the day feel hostile, alien. If we could only have Tony De Luca's pasta on every corner and in every bank line, it would help, maybe. If you feed us, do we not smile? But if you hug us, do we not flinch?

*Winnipeg, Manitoba*

# The Drover Finds It

*A*s I pull out of the apartment's parking lot in Kenora, I punch two of the odometer buttons down to zero. There are three cumulative mileage records on this car, one beyond changing (at least without a mechanic or Dr. Faustus) to keep track of the vehicle's distance-for-life. The other two can be blanked at will, or not. There are three measures of distance for one moving machine; I like that.

My plan is to have one rolling number tell me how far I've gone every day, on this twelve-day solitary ramble to British Columbia and back. The second one will be for the whole trip, and I'm expecting to find a fearful symmetry when I drive back into the yard. For now I aim west, with no symmetry in sight.

\* \* \*

It is difficult to cope with parking outside Winnipeg's River Road house where I once lived, and the difficulty is not only mine. Some of us do the best we can, though, and that is usually almost good enough. Sarah and Jan come out to the car at 10 a.m. and sit jammed together in the front passenger bucket seat. They are friends as well as sisters, and it shows. Sarah has made banana-bread chocolate squares for my trip, a welcome lot of them, arranged carefully in a pan covered with clear wrap.

They have made a card for me, wishing a good trip and congratulating me on being invited to a BC gathering of writers and readers. I save their cards; they are important. On this one, the H on SARAH is suspended, like an afterthought, which we both know it is not.

The kids hug me, and then they go back into the house where I used to live. Sarah rarely looks back and Jan rarely does not, and the only thing I've ever been able to make of this is that we all deal with our realities in our own best ways. I again go to the highway.

I'm close to my father when I'm on the road. On this August day, starting out in clear sky and hot wind, I think that he would approve of the weather and the car and my new sunglasses, and maybe also the cruise control he never got to use because it wasn't here when he still was. He might even approve of my driving, but he probably would be careful to not tell me, or so I remember him. I make a mental note to not make this mistake with my daughters, nor with other people I love, and possibly not even with all the others. We'll see.

The road starts to unwind in the familiar rhythm of radio and highway curves and gas stations and adjustments approximating comfort. I'm home.

\* \* \*

Manitoba and Saskatchewan flow into each other, with the land emphasizing the arbitrary nature of borders. I find the Blue Jays on the radio and for four hours enjoy every pitch and crowd tone as they win 5-4 over the Baltimores, "the other birds" as the play-by-play announcer calls the Orioles. There is absolutely no way I'm going to interrupt the joined flow of highway and ballgame for such trivialities as gas and food, so I let both tanks get down close to empty, then pull over to eat a few well-made banana chocolate squares and listen to the nervous ninth and the post-game show before getting low-octane and soup/sandwich fill-ups.

The prairie highway keeps on flowing west, with me trying to keep up. I'm a passenger as well as a driver, on several levels.

Saskatchewan is dry, with brown grass and leaf-withered trees and shrubs. The CBC news has been telling of the worst drought in fifty years and of the desperation of the farmers. Their despair is ours, whether we know it or not, and whether we like it or not. The aboriginal peoples and the farmers are our key different-angle human links to the land, and our links are breaking. Some of us seem to feel (thought is not dominant) that we can get along without the land, but I can't fathom where such bizarre feelings come from. As the Saskatchewan sun starts to ease off, slanting into my eyes from the unraveling west, I turn to music for direction. Scatter The Mud, an Australian group caught on a prized gift tape, tells me that "the drover finds it hard to change his mind." I repeat this song several times.

I then strike additional dry pay dirt on a tape given to me by my daughters, who know I love the dead-end grief-ridden mea culpa of the Eagles' "Hotel California." I fish the cassette out of the car's right-elbow-rest flip-top cavern and then find the title song, as well as the simplest rewind-to-the-beginning formula. For the next three hours I play the one song nonstop, over and over, no breaks, at increasing volume. I hear and mishear the directions and the angles, memorizing and translating and applying the metaphors to my own stay in the hotel.

*. . . this could be heaven, or it could be hell . . .*

My theory is that all eternal truths are to be found in rock songs, and *yes,* I am a child of the sixties, but I'm also a thoroughly modern neo-conservative dude, a goddamned CEO, in fact.

*. . . we are all prisoners here, of our own device . . .*

The Eagles tell of a "dark desert highway," leading to the place where people have forgotten that we are a part of the land.

*. . . some of us dance to remember, and some dance to forget . . .*

I crank the volume so high that the window glass shimmers, and repeat the song until the echoes are a reflex, heard in advance, felt and understood.

*. . . they wake you up in the middle of the night, those voices from far away . . .*

My hearing loss increases a notch or two, and I've probably scared some wandering roadside coyotes, but it's all worth it. It always is.

*. . . last thing I remember was running for the door, trying to find the way back to where I was before . . .*

This particular sketch of highway is keeping time with the Eagles' bleakly rich vision, no problem, considerable "sweet summer sweat" but no problem.

*. . . you can check out anytime, but you can never leave . . .*

I've never known if the night man is saying "relax" or "good night," and with my progressive hearing deficit it's apt to remain a mystery, just another of life's central imponderables.

*. . . bring your alibis, a nice surprise . . .*

I watch the no-exit prisoners-of-our-own-device scorching sun going down into the gray Camry hood. The colour of the car is officially called "Antique Sage," but I don't think so, especially not as I drive through the desiccated prairie, aiming for Brooks, Alberta, as the place to stop for the night.

*. . . my head was heavy and my sight was dim. I had to stop for the night . . .*

\* \* \*

*I*'ve stopped at Brooks once before, when I had driven to Calgary to watch Jan dance on a Saturday night but then had to leave immediately to get back to Kenora for Monday morning, or so I foolishly thought. My plan then was to drive through the night, tapes and radio and clear sky with full moon to keep me company, but I flat-out couldn't do it. After a very few hours I was getting sleepy, drifting, merging with the moonlight, so I looked for a 2 a.m. rescue at the Holiday Inn Express in Brooks. I was given a huge room, quiet halls, comfortable bed, thick towels, coffee maker in the room plus a grandiose and "free" self-serve breakfast in the lobby promised for the morning. I was rescued.

The only problem arose the next morning as I left the building to discover that the world smelled bad, as if overnight it had died and gone to rot. The odour was fierce and penetrating, but in spite of being curious I decided to leave it alone, to not look the rescuing town in the orifice. I drove away.

On this new trip I pull into Brooks after driving 1,200 kilometres on the dry, hot day, noting the absence of grim odour anywhere in my vicinity. I accept with appropriate gratitude a much better room than all of those which Medicine Hat had so cavalierly filled before I arrived. Sleep is good, not as good as movement, but definitely good.

In the morning, I decide to give Brooks a second chance, olfactory-wise. I put on sneakers, shorts and a tank top and wander the outskirts. The world smells just fine. Off on a side road there is a tucked away pond-side park, with several pelicans alternating between fishing deep and ambling the surface. They ignore me with ease, my neophyte species being so obviously and completely inferior to their pterodactyl heritage. They own the pond, and they know it. I have no objection to their arrogance, they've earned it, so I am content to gape and admire as they inspect the top and underside of their water property.

The Brooks park has a wooden observation platform and a near-by paved road with almost no traffic. There is a fence placed between the quiet road and the overpass leading back to the hotel, but to what purpose? Possibly, the obstacle is to deter aging walkers and prehistoric pelicans. I climb the fence, a creaky version of no-problem, and go back to the Holiday Inn to check out, glad I made the choice to give Brooks a second whiff.

\* \* \*

I've got my oft-cursed cell phone with me and even have it turned on (this is rare), just in case someone who might care for me chooses to call. The little TV-screen face of this plastic-wood-covered phone has a capital B followed by a flashing-on-and-off tiny house, then ABC in a rectangle (these are total mysteries to me, but must be meaningful, Nokia being global and rich and famous), bars of graduated intensity to the right and left of the screen, *and* the word ROAMING at mid-screen. A word to live by.

\* \* \*

While the Eagles' rhapsodic vision of mobile doom seemed apt for the drought of Saskatchewan and eastern Alberta, it doesn't fit the Rockies, not for me. As I get into the high foothills near Dead Man's Flats (and I freely admit that on several occasions I've thought of mailing myself a postcard from there, with the text being, "Dear Peter – I *told* you to never stop here! Goodbye, Pete") and then go toward Canmore and the familiar streets of Banff, I switch to another tape, William Ackerman's ethereal tones of *Winter*. It's hot again today, at +28°C in Banff, but Ackerman's drifting cool nevertheless seems to match the aloof mountains, layer on layer.

There are some old and new friends to visit in Banff, not people but places. I take the walking path along the edge of the Bow River, then up the slanted hillside route up to the Banff Centre. I can't go to the paths of Leighton Studios because I'm here now as a watcher, not a writer. Then I take a rambling circuitous route back to the main street and go to the bookstore, wander the aisles and buy a few so the Antique Sage will have a library, and detour to the tourist-acclimated Post Office to mail a book to Sarah and Jan, before drifting to and sitting down weary at the bar in Coyote's restaurant. There, I drink several dark beer and eat great food while I watch the chef do his rapid-fire multi-task wizardry and rejoice over not having any responsibility other than treating dark beer with the respect it deserves.

Later, the Mount Royal Hotel takes me in, giving me room #247 with the scary ease of those who routinely save lives, as if it's just an insignificant part of their humdrum daily ritual. We set up these social-role games, complex and fluctuating, and it's all I can do to keep up. I collapse in room 247, to sleep off a few of the complexities.

\* \* \*

The next day I cruise low speed through the Rockies toward Radium Hot Springs, playing William Ackerman again and ignoring the frantic truckers and BC non-truckers behind me and in a hurry to get home. "If you're in a rush, fly WestJet, psycho," I say to the rabid trucker looming in my rear-view mirror, himself trailed in close formation by twenty-six pseudo-laidback BC folk in full-drag SUVs. I'm doing 95 in a 90-km/hr zone. To hell with them I say, and then I say it again, flipping the rear-view mirror into night-blind and cranking up Billy A to majestic levels of wispy escapism.

When I get to Kootenay National Park in BC, I get lost at Radium Junction, confused by the crush of traffic in the madness of noon-hour, so I pull into a campground, spot Buddy sitting in a folding chair facing the highway traffic and the sun, park the Antique Sage a respectful distance away and stroll on over. "Trucks are some damn slow on that Highway 93," I open. He grins, looking happy and aware of the world, sitting there in his tanned face and arms and lower legs, with his white belly and chest preparing to surge into pink.

"Yeah, they *are* a cautious lot. You lost?" he says, looking over at my Ontario plates.

"No, I don't think so. This *is* Scarborough, right?"

By now, he's sitting up straighter, enjoying himself. Antique Sage and I roam the highways, looking for geezers in bored distress, intent on bringing jocularity into every pre-sunburned life we can find.

"You're a bit west of it. When you get to Vancouver, hang a hard-about right turn and you'll be on track."

"I truly am lost. Which is the best way to Vancouver?"

"Do you want scenic? If so, keep going the way you were before you turned in here. You'll go through wonderful country just above the American border, Highway Number 3. If you're in a hurry, go back the other way and you'll eventually come to Kamloops and then the Coquihalla Highway to Hope, it's toll, and then it's just a skip into Vancouver."

"I think I'll take the scenic route. Thanks. You from here?"

"From Calgary. Just wander around BC every summer. We like the campgrounds, and I like sitting where I can watch the traffic. Find it restful. You on business?"

"Nope, just cruising around, like you." We talk some more, wishing each other good trips, good lives in a way, and off I go. "Thanks for the directions. Bye."

After I aim south along winding roads, through valleys and beside thick woods and occasional lakes, past Skookumchuk and Wasa and Cranbrook and Moyie Lake, I find that Bill Ackerman has lost the rhythm of the road, of this particular road. I pull over to rummage through my tapes. Leo Kottke's *Peculiaroso* comes to hand. When in BC, be *as* BC. I do admire Leo, especially his quirky highway-friendly ironies and warts.

\* \* \*

*T*he next day is hot, burning wind on your face hot, and there are forest fires in the area. I buy a large box of cherries at a roadside stand near Osoyoos and then pull over at a *scenic viewpoint* high and directly above the town, so I can eat the cherries and stop the world from moving by the ploy of sitting still and outside, and by letting the air-conditioning wash off me in my own sweet summer sweat. I sit on a tire-stopping cement curb eating cherries and saying Osoyoos many times, to capture all those connected round vowels in my imagination. I also admire the town and valley and river-lakes, from high up.

Just off to the right of the moderately narrow dirt pullover-to-admire-the-view place is another even higher hill, with a house stilted on the hill's steep slanting side, so that the back of the house is almost buried in hill and the front deck is sticking out into space. I conclude that the house is level, and the hill is not. There is a sign in the parking area, advertising this Bed and Breakfast hillside home. I make a note, in the mind's eye, to come back, to stay or to buy it.

Two motorcycles pull over, and large men wearing leather, tattoos and beaten-up helmets get off, looking hot and tired. "Wow!" one says, nodding at me and looking out at the view. The other man comes over to the edge, where I'm tossing cherry pits out into rootless oblivion, and he looks over the valley, more restrained than his friend, but involved. He's into this, too. He spots the hillside B & B, stares at it for a while, and then says to the world at large and to himself, "*That* is my house." I look up from my cherry and stillness reverie, still sitting on the low concrete tire-stopper thing, and say,

"Nope. It can't be. I got here first and claimed it, ten minutes ago. You'll have to go through me to get it." The two guys look at me, then look at each other, and start to laugh, but with deep fearful respect is how I read it. "Oh, damn," the second one says, "I guess we'll have to keep on looking." "Good," I say. "Want some cherries?" They do. Osoyoos keeps on shimmering in the heat, way down there, and I keep on working on the round vowels.

I leave first, with Kottke's *Peculiaroso* still keeping finger-pickin'-good time with the unfolding of the countryside. There are miles to go, to Vancouver, before I sleep.

\* \* \*

As I approach Vancouver the highway widens and the speed and number of cars increases. I get nervous. Urban driving makes me nervous, or to be more quantitatively accurate, it scares the living hell out of me. In fact, I get fully a-scared driving in any community larger than Seal Cove on Grand Manan Island, which has a population of 550, if Deep Cove is included.

There are no signs that I'm able to spot telling me where to turn off to get to the downtown West End Stanley Park area of Vancouver, so I end up being carried across the bridge into North Vancouver, shaking my head at my inept self. I get badly turned around in construction and become fearful of inadvertently going back to Radium Junction. I could *not* deal with Buddy in the trailer park. The loss of face would be devastating. I stop by some recuperating highway construction workers to ask directions. They glance at my Ontario plates. I decide to skip my isn't-this-Scarborough? routine, on the slim chance they've heard it before, so instead play it straight and ask for the Lion's Gate Bridge. They tell me, with detectable ironic disdain for my Ontario-based incompetence. I follow directions perfectly, easing over the narrow, old, wobbly, and under-construction scenic bridge into Stanley Park.

The construction guys had warned me that it is Fireworks Night and there may be a few extra people around, so I'm not surprised when there's a cop at the corner of Denman who won't let me (or anyone else) turn off, saying I "have to go around" to get to the Sylvia Hotel. I want to ask, "around what? around where? around how?" but he waves me off. I can sense a rising hallelujah chorus of those who are rejoicing in the fact that they are not with me right now: kids, friends, partners, ex-partners, acquaintances, fifth cousins; they're all glad I'm alone to be told to "go around." I give the chorus a mid-finger salute, but this only inflames its rhapsodic tones.

I do as I'm told, as always, and then there's another cop-guarded barricade. I wait for Cop #2 to look my way so I can ask what do I *do* here, but he isn't looking. I start to go around the barricade because there's room to do so, so it must be ok. Cop #2's radar kicks in, and he goes storm trooper berserk, yelling at me to stop. I stop. He says, "What in hell are you doing?"

"I want to get to the Sylvia, so I can check in. I couldn't get your attention."

"Did the barricade not get your attention? Back up and get out of here."

"I can't go to the Sylvia?"

"That's right, genius. Now, get out of here."

So I claim Ontario exhaustion, and losing battles with bikers and truckers and getting lost in North Vancouver and am working myself up to a genuine tearful antique sage collapse when he says, "Oh, for God's sake, go on. But don't *ever* go around my barricade again," and then he walks away. That went well, I think, giving the steering wheel a victorious high five as I pick my automotive way toward the Sylvia amongst annoyed middle-of-the-street pedestrians.

However, I gloated too soon, as the entryway to the hotel's street is also blocked off and security guards will *not* let me go around, fake tears be damned. I back up two blocks, pull the car up onto the sidewalk and drive along it for a few minutes, going slowly so as not to injure or otherwise inconvenience the crowds of pedestrians. Peculiaroso is as peculiaroso does, I always say, and as I lower Antique Sage off the sidewalk a smiling woman of my approximate age gives me a well-deserved round of applause. She's in love, and I don't blame her one bit.

I check into the Sylvia, get on my walking-to-fireworks clothes, (sneakers and shorts and sparkly-clean tank top), and go back over Denman. I blow a kiss to the puzzled barricade-fetishist Cop #2, who doesn't recognize me from Eve. Then I walk the ten-kilometre seawall, watch the fireworks, eat street-vendor food, and feel more urbane than I usually do. All of this is good, even the detestable urbanity.

Room #405 at the Sylvia accepts me into its closet-size grandeur without a qualm. I've proven my mettle.

\* \* \*

Eight days later, I ease back into my yard in Kenora and check my rolling odometer. It's at 5,848, but the symmetry escapes me. I'll have to make more trips to see if I can catch the drift of the coordinates, later.

*The Sylvia Hotel*
*Vancouver, British Columbia*

# *Interesting Movement*

*I*'m walking the seawall at Stanley Park, Vancouver, and I cannot recognize what is feeling so familiar. The seawall walk itself is well known to me, a twelve-kilometre winding circle from the Sylvia Hotel on English Bay, around the water's edge wall to the Westin Bayshore Hotel, then up and over Denman and back to the Sylvia. The feeling of this day's familiarity is not due to the many other times I've taken this walk. This is something different. I try to identify the sensation by going blank, walking and observing without thinking, assuming from past practice that the recognition will flip into clear view when it wants to, if it wants to.

It does. What I'm sensing is an extension, a continuation of a contemporary dance piece from several weeks before. Ben and I had driven from Winnipeg to Calgary to watch Jan perform in a piece called "Coming & Going, Doing & Being," choreographed by Anne Flynn. Jan studies dance at the University of Calgary, and I had been looking forward to seeing her in this piece, partly so I can get a better feel for the University of Calgary perspective but primarily just to watch Jan. She warms my heart.

Ben and I watched the dance on two nights, and it was very different each time. The piece was improvisational, with few guidelines having been given to the twelve performers by the choreographer. These weren't announced to the audience, which was left to its own devices, but Jan had explained it to us in advance. The rules were these: the stage was divided, by imagination, into lanes running from side to side, wing to wing, with six lanes each about a metre in width. The dancers were not to touch or speak to each other or change lanes while on stage, but otherwise they were on their own. They could run or walk or crawl, move forwards or backwards, stand in the wings off stage or be on stage the whole time, and they could interact with others or be solitary. They could come and go, do and be, as they saw fit, as we do with our daily rounds, making it up as we go along within certain ill-defined and fluid but nevertheless definite limits.

On the first night the piece was light, varying from almost-frantic to casual-happy, with the performers' interactions often being amusing and with even the introspective and serious portions avoiding sombre or disturbing tones. It was fun but not particularly moving, a clever idea and that was all.

The next night came from another place, and I found myself leaning forward, caught, for much of the twenty-five-minute performance. I watched my daughter and another woman get into a spontaneous interaction that made me hold my breath. They began by slowly crawling towards each other, with differing attitudes of confidence or tentative purpose. For several minutes they moved closer and closer, then backed off to sit and face each other, finally looking away as they appeared to decide to retreat only to change their minds and come back, closer yet. They were connected, and conflicted. The scene was one of generous physical tension, an approach/avoid masterpiece. I saw that my daughter is an adult and a fascinating one but was not surprised, having suspected this for some time.

In the other lanes some of the performers were running, being chased or moving solitary and wild, while others were simply walking in their lanes, pondering, until confronted by another at which time decisions were necessary. Would they acknowledge each other and interact, and if not who would back away and give up the lane? Some dancers sought out intimate face-to-face positions, while others avoided this and could be seen finding a lane of their own, for a few solitary moments. The overall mood was pensive and somewhat dark, with a pushing edge of abandon. I was glad to have seen both nights, for the balance and the relief they gave each other.

After the show, I eavesdropped on an audience member talking at the choreographer. He was complaining that the performance wasn't really dance at all, "just interesting movement." Anne Flynn barely suppressed a sigh as she replied, saying that she feels that is precisely what dance *is*, interesting movement.

I think about this as I walk the seawall on a bright March morning, catching the connection. We have self-assigned lanes as we move along the water's edge, the walkers and runners and bicyclists and roller-bladers. Decisions have to be made over and over again, as to who will give way and who will stay firm. There is rarely an exchange of speech between strangers and never a touch, but eyes do flick to strange eyes, usually quickly darting away but not always. Rarely eyes and face will smile, and on this twelve-kilometre walk involving hundreds of passages of strangers with lane-based interactive decisions, I count four verbal "good mornings" and about ten nods with eye-smiles.

One huge lumbering jogger bangs me with his arm as he veers into my path, aggressive and uncaring in his big-beast dominant territoriality. I wish him a fall that breaks some vital part, acknowledging with the curse that a broken social contract is also a two-way lane.

Most bicyclists dismount where the signs say they must, but a few do not, oblivious or deviant, either way being beyond the rules, outside the tribe. Many people pretend that you do not exist as you walk by, marking you as invisible or low-caste or dangerous, while others' eyes harden, defiant with a presence too near. We carve out our own weaving lanes, on the seawall and in our minds.

This walk, a familiar and necessary part of my life, has just been given a new dimension, a varying interpretation. I feel relieved that I was able to see it and am pleased with the recurring vision of the dance. I'd like to thank Anne Flynn for this view of how we weave by each other, coming and going, but I'll probably never get near her lane. I will, however, be able to thank Jan, as our lanes connect.

*The Sylvia Hotel*
*Vancouver, British Columbia*

# *A Cure for Mobility*

*T*wo of us are planning on having supper at the Riverview Lodge in Dryden, Ontario. We are both mobile types, and it has taken us a while to get here. Heather is from Dryden, as a kid, and since that time she has moved around, to Africa, then to the Northwest Territories, where we worked together, then to Hawaii, and now to her present home in Tasmania, Australia. I'm from Nova Scotia and also have been away and on the road, but I still remember that the evening meal is called "supper," except on special "dinner" occasions, when you dress up and lose your sense of ease. We're here for supper.

It's a warm June evening, before the full force of bugs and the occasional tourists arrive, and there's not a whiff of paper-mill odour in the air as we walk slowly to and then from "The Lodge." Heather is showing me the places where she grew up, their changes and mostly their sameness, as we stroll the evening streets. We're enjoying ourselves, twenty-year friends sharing time and space.

Heather stops in front of a two-story house, which has a tree and shrub tunnel-lane leading to the unused front door. It is easy to tell that it is unused, as the step is littered with tree twigs and general vegetative debris and the leafy tunnel itself blocks easy access to the door. This is a back-door house, one where the evening meal probably is called supper, the same sort of house I once knew and may again if I ever get control of this mobility attitude.

Heather says she wants me to meet someone, and as we go in the back door without knocking, she is helloing, speaking loudly and warmly. We're greeted by a white-haired woman, and Heather introduces us, using the word "Aunt" for the woman who firmly shakes my hand and firmly sizes me up. We sit in the living room to talk, to meet. The TV gets turned off from the news, without hesitation. I like this person. Heather explains the relationship, which is complicated and semi-distant, as Heather's mother's uncle's sister was this woman's cousin, or some such. I ignore these familial convolutions, but I do get the central point. This is a much loved and honoured woman, Heather's aunt. I learn some details: she is ninety-four and lives alone for most of the year, and this has been her home since 1927. "The year Babe Ruth hit sixty home runs," I offer, but it's not caught, or maybe she's an Aaron or McQuire or Bonds fan.

There is a wonderfully evocative oil painting of a part of the side of her house, unframed and propped on a low table. It shows the depths and colours of a real home, roof and door, red-leafed ivy on white paint, and green trees and shrubs at the edges. I love it. Someone has cared about angles and shades including those on the concept of home.

Heather and her aunt talk back and forth, volleying details and comparing plans, as aunts and nieces can do, even if they aren't related. I mostly listen and watch, feeling comfortable in this place that is so thick and alive with memories and absent people. These recollections and absences are openly cherished, so they give the house texture and humour and ongoing life, not a sense of loss. If I pay attention, I might learn something here.

I become totally captive to the moment when Heather's aunt says she's going for a driver's test this week, as the government people insist on this "every two years, since I turned eighty." She is not worried about the test, and I'm surprised to notice that I'm not either.

As Heather and I walk back to our temporary homes, following our own uneven spirals, we're enjoying ourselves even more. We've just been shown the cure for mobility, which may prove useful if we ever decide we need it, and if we are willing to take it.

*Dryden, Ontario*